SUSTAINABLE MINIMALISM

ZERO WASTE

Minimalist Habits for A Simpler Life

AMY LANDRY

Copyright © 2022 Amy Landry

All rights reserved. No part of this publication may be reproduced, distributed, or transmitted in any form or by any means, including photocopying, recording, or other electronic or mechanical methods, without the prior written permission of the publisher, except in the case of brief quotations embodied in critical reviews and certain other non-commercial uses permitted by copyright law.

TABLE OF CONTENTS

INTRODUCTION 1
    WHAT IS MINIMALISM? 1
    HOW TO PUT MINIMALISM INTO PRACTICE 2
    PROJECT 333 2
    MINIMALIST RACE 3
    BENEFITS OF MINIMALISM 3
    THE HOUSE IS THE PLACE WHERE MOST OF THE TIME THIS JOURNEY OF DISCOVERY BEGAN 4
    MINIMALISM AT HOME HELPS YOU ORGANIZE THE DOMESTIC MANAGEMENT 5
    MINIMALISM AT HOME HELPS YOU TO CHOOSE THE SUITABLE MATERIALS 6
    MINIMALISM AT HOME HELPS YOU REDUCE WASTE 6
    MINIMALISM AT HOME HELPS YOU TO FEEL SUSTAINABLE 7
    MINIMALISM AT HOME HELPS YOU TO MAKE SPECIAL ENCOUNTERS 7
    MINIMALISM AT HOME HELPS YOU DRESS CONSCIOUSLY 7
    HOW TO FIND THE STYLE THAT SUITS YOU BEST? 8

CHAPTER 1 9

WHAT IS SUSTAINABLE MINIMALISM? 9
    A BRIEF HISTORY OF MINIMALISM 9
    MINIMALISM AS A WAY OF LIFE 10

CHAPTER 2 19

MINIMALISM: THE FIRST STEP TOWARDS A SUSTAINABLE LIFESTYLE 19
    SIMPLIFY OUR LIFE 20
    4 STEPS TO START A MINIMALIST LIFE 22

CHAPTER 3 24

THE DIDEROT EFFECT: WHY WE BUY OBJECTS WE DON'T NEED 24
    DIDEROT EFFECT: THE TERM COINED IN THE TWENTIETH CENTURY BY GRANT MCCRACKEN 25

CHAPTER 4 27

BECOMING AWARE CONSUMERS 27
    CONSCIOUS CONSUMERS: HOW DO YOU BECOME? 27

CONSCIOUS CONSUMERS BREAKING DOWN THE BARRIER OF IMMEDIATE SATISFACTION 27
BUT HOW DO YOU BECOME A RESPONSIBLE CONSUMER? 29
A PRACTICAL GUIDE TO THE RESPONSIBLE CONSUMER 29

CHAPTER 5 33

LESS PLASTIC 33

REDUCE PLASTIC WASTE IN 14 STEPS 33

CHAPTER 6 37

THE CARBON FOOTPRINT 37

THE CARBON FOOTPRINT 37
START REDUCING YOUR CARBON FOOTPRINT 37
HOW TO CALCULATE THE CARBON FOOTPRINT 38
PRODUCT LIFE CYCLE PHASES 39
CALCULATION OF THE CARBON FOOTPRINT GENERATED BY AN ORGANIZATION ... 40

CHAPTER 7 42

DIFFERENCE BETWEEN SUSTAINABILITY AND MINIMALISM 42

WHAT IS SUSTAINABILITY? 43

CHAPTER 8 46

THE DECLUTTERING 46

WHAT TO DO? 46
WHAT IS DECLUTTERING? 46
HOW TO KEEP THE RESULTS OVER TIME? 54
BATHROOM IDEA 54
WARDROBE IDEA 55
CLOSET IDEA 55
KITCHEN IDEA 55
10 TIPS FOR TIDYING UP 55

CHAPTER 9 57

MARIE KONDO 'S RULES FOR HOME DECLUTTERING 57

EVERYTHING AT ONCE 58
CLOTHES 59
BOOKS 60
SHEETS, SLIPS, AND SCATTERED PAPERS 61

- Tidying up the cupboard 63
- Closet decluttering... 63
- Geraline Thomas decluttering rules 64
- Not doing this is just an excuse 64
- Reorganize spaces and tidy up the house 64

CHAPTER 10 66

HOW TO ORGANIZE YOUR CLOSET WITH THE SSO METHOD (EMPTY, SELECT AND THEN ORGANIZE) 66

- The SSO method: clear select and then organize 67

CHAPTER 11 71

20 MINIMALIST HABITS FOR A SIMPLER LIFE............................. 71

- The minimalist habits that change your life 71

CHAPTER 12 77

HOW TO SAVE WITH MINIMALISM 77

- What is a minimalist budget?.. 77
- The rules for saving with minimalism 78
- Caffeine - Detox 83

CHAPTER 13 86

TEACHING SUSTAINABLE MINIMALISM TO CHILDREN 86

- Why teach children about minimalism? 86
- Why should you teach children about minimalism? 87
- In summary: why teach children about minimalism? 91
- I happily embraced a simpler approach............................ 92
- Let them play alone without anxiety 93
- Let them create 93
- Let them rest 93
- Rest must become a priority, not a luxury. 94
- Let them solve 94

CHAPTER 14 97

CREATING A MINIMAL WARDROBE FOR CHILDREN 97

- Steps 98

CHAPTER 15 104

CAPSULE WARDROBE: A NEW APPROACH TO WARDROBE **104**

5 TIPS **105**

CHAPTER 16 .... **107**

BE MINIMALIST EVERY DAY **107**

    CLOTHING, SHOES, AND ACCESSORIES 107
    FOOD 109
    WORK EQUIPMENT 109
    FURNITURE, FURNISHINGS, AND ACCESSORIES FOR THE HOME 110
    MOBILE APP 110
    APPS AND PROGRAMS FOR THE PC 111
    LEISURE AND PLAYFUL ACTIVITIES 111
    SOCIAL MEDIA 112
    PRINCIPLE OF IMPROVEMENT BY SUBTRACTION APPLIED TO LIFE 113
    MINIMALISM AND MIND 115
    MINIMALISM AND BODY 116
    PURCHASES TO IMPROVE, COMPENSATE, COVER MINIMALISM, AND ACCEPTANCE 116

CHAPTER 17 .... **119**

MINIMALISM SKINCARE **119**

    WHAT HAPPENS WHEN THIS ATTITUDE APPLIES TO SKINCARE? 119
    BUT THE SKIN DOES MINIMALISM WORK? CAN A MINIMALIST ROUTINE WORK ON THE SKIN?
    120
    THE REAL NEEDS OF THE SKIN 120
    THE MUST-HAVE PRODUCTS IN SKINCARE 121

CHAPTER 18 .... **122**

MAKE-UP DECLUTTERING **122**

    WHAT IS DECLUTTERING MAKE-UP FOR? HOW TO CHOOSE WHAT TO KEEP AND WHAT TO THROW? 122
    WHY DO DECLUTTERING MAKE-UP? WHAT IS IT FOR REORGANIZING THE TRICKS? 123
    HOW TO SET THE DECLUTTERING MAKE-UP: WHAT TO HAVE AVAILABLE TO START THE MAKE-UP MAKE-UP 124
    IN ADDITION TO THE ESSENTIALS, WE ALSO KEEP EXTRAORDINARY PRODUCTS FOR MORE PARTICULAR LOOKS 126
    CONCLUDE THE DECLUTTERING: IN ORDER NOT TO CREATE DISORDER, WE USE ORGANIZER AND WE HAVE EVERYTHING WITH CRITERIA 126

CHAPTER 19 .... **128**

APPLY MINIMALISM TO THE KITCHEN **128**
  THE AIM IS NOT TO WASTE 129
  COOKING IS IN ITSELF A MINIMALIST ART 129
  STUDY, SEARCH, LEARN, EXPERIMENT WITHOUT LOSING YOUR MIND 134

CHAPTER 20 .... **135**

THE THOUGHT OF FUMIO SASAKI **135**
  WHO IS FUMIO SASAKI ? 135
  BECAUSE THIS BOOK IS FOR YOU 136

CHAPTER 21 .... **138**

CONCLUSIONS **138**
  WHAT IS MINIMALISM? 139
  USE THE THINGS YOU LOVE. IF YOU CAN FIX WHAT IS NOT WORKING PROPERLY 141
  CUT OUT UNNECESSARY AND HARMFUL ACTIVITIES 142
  USE THE TIME FOR WHAT YOU ENJOY DOING 143
  MANAGE PERSONAL RELATIONSHIPS 143
  CHOOSE CAREFULLY WHO TO DEDICATE YOURSELF TO 144
  WHEN YOU RELAX, YOU RELAX 144
  IMPROVE SLEEP 145
  IMPROVE NUTRITION 145
  EXERCISE (OR SOMETHING SIMILAR) 145
  WHAT HAPPENS ONCE WE HAVE DONE ALL OF THIS? 146

INTRODUCTION

Look around you and take an inventory of the objects you see. Do you have the feeling that there are many things accumulated? More than what you need? Are you one of those women who have a huge bag that you haven't seen the bottom of for some time? Do you have clothes you haven't worn for over a year now? Kitchen utensils that you have only used once?

We live in a world where it is normal to stockpile more items than you need, be it office tools, clothes, shoes, make-up, tools, etc. These objects take up physical space in our homes, they mess up wardrobes, chests of drawers, chests, shoe racks, etc. But the worst thing is that they also occupy our mental space and our time since we have to classify, order, and clean them.

Well, there is a philosophy of life that can help you see and manage this accumulation of things differently. Let's talk about minimalism. Minimalism is not about having less, but about making room for what matters.

What is minimalism?

The idea is to live with the bare minimum, which for each of us is based on our life circumstances, and differences to have fewer things, to have more physical and mental space. In the process of reflecting on why we accumulate objects that we don't use, we will realize that there are many reasons of an emotional nature, in addition to the typical "if I ever need to".

Clothes, gifts, letters that we are unable to get rid of because they remind us of moments from the past as if memories were hidden in material objects. Minimalism is an exercise that helps us separate from material objects and realize that memories live within us, not in objects. The less you need, the freer you will be.

How to put minimalism into practice

The ideal is to start a little at a time, divide the objects into categories and evaluate what you need, which objects you are not sure you need and which ones you are sure you want to discard.

In the kitchen: what are the kitchen utensils you haven't used for more than a year? Do you use all the spices you have?

In the closet: what clothes or shoes are no longer fit or have not been used for more than a year?

In the study: do you have notebooks, old diaries, notes that date back to years ago, or drawers that you practically never open?

There are a few challenges that can help you put minimalism into practice:

Project 333

Project 333 invites us to choose 33 items of clothing (it is not necessary to throw the others away, just put them aside) and spend 3 months using only those. So we will realize how little we need to get dressed and how much time we save choosing what to wear since we don't have much to choose from.

Minimalist race

Another challenge is to agree with someone who is going through the same process to embark on a kind of minimalist contest. On the first day of the month, both of you will have to get rid of something you own; the second day of two objects; the third day of three objects; and so on until the thirtieth day. Whoever manages to resist longer wins. Once you have your heap of items to get rid of, you can donate many or sell them to second-hand shops.

Benefits of minimalism

I. It helps us keep the house tidy and get rid of "junk".
II. There is a new way of understanding minimalism in the home.
III. It is no longer the simple aseptic design stream that looks like it just came out of a magazine.
IV. More people are finding great benefits from the minimalist lifestyle, whose basic concept is to eliminate excesses, what annoys, what is no longer needed to make room for what you like, is useful, and makes you feel good.
V. So this way also invests in other fields, both at home and outside, not only from an aesthetic point of view, thanks to a much broader and more complete vision.
VI. It is a matter of reducing the numerous commitments you have during the day to the essentials, better selecting the people you frequent, eliminating harmful foods, using products that do not

harm your body or the environment ... but it is not limited only to this.

VII. Minimalism pushes you to focus attention on one thing at a time and makes you fully understand the importance of time since you are the only one who decides what is the best way to spend it, since we all have 24 hours available in one. day.

VIII. From here an inner analysis automatically arises to understand exactly how to make the most of the time left to live.

"Live every day as if it were your last and ... one day you will get it right"

-Woody Allen

When you then start living according to your priorities, you will wonder why you didn't start doing it sooner.

The house is the place where most of the time this journey of discovery began

It often comes at first the has frustration of clutter and the awareness of having too many things. Then the decision to eliminate the superfluous and to bring order. And hence the infinite happiness and satisfaction for having found peace by creating more space in the house.

Your mind sometimes resists change:

- ✓ "It might take one day."
- ✓ " I paid very much for him, it would be a shame"
- ✓ "It's a gift!"
- ✓ "I used to like it, it suited me well"

You have to answer in kind:

- ✓ "How long has it been since I last used it?"
- ✓ "Can I sell it?"
- ✓ "Do I need it or could it be useful to someone else?"
- ✓ "Now I like it, is it okay?"
- ✓ "It works? Is broken?"

This reasoning can equally apply to many aspects of life at home:

- ✓ Cohabitants
- ✓ Daily commitments
- ✓ The food you put on the table
- ✓ The clothes you wear
- ✓ The materials you surround yourself with
- ✓ Products to clean the house
- ✓ Personal hygiene products

Use these tools to find the most suitable one:

- ✓ Weekly menu
- ✓ To-do list
- ✓ Bullet journal
- ✓ Fly lady method
- ✓ Kondo method

Minimalism at home helps you organize the domestic management

A minimalist home allows you to simplify everyday organizational management as much as possible. An organized life is essential to face the days more peacefully and serenely, and you can optimize space and time. The organization is a tool that, if used with flexibility and kindness, can improve your daily life.

There are 4 main factors which if well managed and balanced can help reduce stress:

- ✓ Space
- ✓ Weather
- ✓ Money
- ✓ Resources (physical and mental energies)

Learning to be organized is possible at any age, so it's never too late (or too early) to start.

Minimalism at home helps you to choose the suitable materials

The materials you surround yourself with contribute to your well-being, especially at home. If you use natural materials you can reduce the level of pollution inside your home.

Minimalism at home helps you reduce waste

Can you lead a life without producing waste? Once you start thinking differently, then your habits change too, and little by little, you feel involved in helping to improve the world you live in, without necessarily having to upset your days.

These are the "5 Rs" indispensable for sustainable waste management:

- ✓ Reduce
- ✓ Reuse
- ✓ Recycle

- ✓ Collect
- ✓ Recover

Minimalism at home helps you to feel sustainable

Do we know the quality (and quantity) of the food we bring indoors and to our table?

Minimalism in the kitchen could result in:

- ✓ Prepare simple dishes, not too elaborate, quick, and easy to make, (especially for everyday life or for those with small children who do not want to spend all their time cooking)
- ✓ Pay attention to waste and therefore, for example, reuse food scraps to cook new dishes.
- ✓ Reduce excesses, avoiding big binges, but also not buying more food than necessary, risking making it expire.
- ✓ Prefer quality over quantity, through the careful choice of the foods that are brought to the table

Minimalism at home helps you to make special encounters

However, it is not always possible to organize a party at home or it happens to get discouraged by the amount of work that must be faced to prepare everything, with the terror that a disaster will emerge.

Minimalism at home helps you dress consciously

STYLE is a way to communicate one's identity, manifesting it through the choice of furniture, a dress, behavior, or anything else.

ELEGANCE represents research and attention to detail, with care and full consideration for oneself.

In practice, being able to show who you are with simplicity and authenticity, to live more peacefully. When you wear the clothes that you like and that represent you, then you look good and you are happy, this also happens with the house.

How to find the style that suits you best?

Simply by getting to know you, investigating your tastes, experimenting, and training yourself to perceive your feelings and emotions. Not surprisingly, most people who approach minimalism do so after having freed and lightened the wardrobe from all those clothes that no longer represent them, they feel truly satisfied and regenerated.

To apply these principles you must:

- ✓ Organize life at home
- ✓ Living small
- ✓ Choose natural materials
- ✓ Reduce waste
- ✓ Feed yourself sustainably
- ✓ Carry out special meetings
- ✓ Dress consciously

CHAPTER 1
WHAT IS SUSTAINABLE MINIMALISM?

Minimalism is a happily polysemantic term that embraces many areas of our knowledge, which in history has come into contact with architecture, design, literature, cinema, music, and many other artistic spheres.

A brief history of minimalism

At the level of the figurative arts, it was in the 1950s that the new minimalist current took hold, based on the belief that art has its reality, which is therefore not an imitation of that reality.

First, it is an artist like Frank Stella who exhibited the Black Paintings in 1959 at the MoMA and proposes a new way of thinking and living art, against an elitist tendency to understand the work of art. Others after him, Morris, Judd, LeWitt, readjust the concept to the sphere of design, towards a deliberate absence of expression, to give due importance to focusing on the single artistic object: linear and repeated geometric shapes, single objects that were as neutral and impersonal as possible.

In 1974, on the other hand, minimalism reached the musical sphere, with pianist Michael Nyman coining the expression minimal music. Among its various artistic applications, the concept of minimalism is characterized by less is more.

Minimalism as a way of life

Here I would like to talk more precisely about minimalism as a lifestyle, that is, I would like to bring the discourse back to a level that is delicately ethical-philosophical, restricting the great container of the concept of Minimalism to the sphere of your personal daily life. So let's try to see how it is possible to assume a minimalist belief and see how it can help you reach an inner serenity that will healthily lighten your quiet life.

Although with other denominations, the convinced fight against vices, surplus, and the desire to reduce the superfluous to understand more intimate and fundamental parts of one's self is a concept that has its roots since the period of great classicism.

The desire to move away from the futile and to agree on inner serenity has been constant prerogatives of the man who starts from the dawn of civilization and then passes from the advent of the industrial revolution; with the establishment of consumerism and its new cultural paradigm that tends to commodify the individuality itself, the minimalist belief as a lifestyle has taken hold more and more, up to today on this site, with this proposal.

Minimalism as a lifestyle is a way of thinking that embraces simplicity and tries to move away from easy consumerism, it is an attitude that is not forced deprivation, but acceptance of what we are emotionally linked to. It is therefore not a simple and bland operation. Proceed by points and you will see that, armed with your willpower, you too will be able to free yourself from material and emotional surplus.

1. **Focus on one thing at a time**

What Is Sustainable Minimalism?

Yes, trying to embrace this lifestyle is certainly a delicate operation, but don't lose heart, the hardest part is the initial one. So where to start? The first point is to clarify yourself; take a break and focus, remove all thoughts and distractions and take stock of the situation.

Are you thinking of the neighbor who asked you for the oil he was missing? Greet him momentarily and be quiet around you. Becoming minimalist involves facing one thing at a time calmly and without other thoughts, first breakfast, then working hours, then going out with friends.

Let the others be multi-tasking, allow yourself the calm and serenity, just like the minimalists of the Sixties: a single object, clear and linear. Do you want to become minimalist? it can be done, first make yourself mentally comfortable to do it.

2. Evaluate your space and review your priorities

Finally ready, calm, focused, and examine your space. What have you surrounded yourself with over the years? Not that you've exaggerated maniacally with anything in particular, but try to reconsider your actual priorities! What do you feel you need? Or, what are you honestly pleased to have with you?

Take a step back and look around. How many items are stacked on your desk? How many business cards from ten thousand different restaurants are hanging on your bulletin board? And all those pens and pencils, all those markers?

Maybe if you only had one, if you only had one poster, only one or two photos, and only one cup in the kitchen you might feel more fulfilled and differently for all those precise objects that are the cup I recognize.

3. **Decluttering in every area of your home**

   Then start by doing a decluttering operation in all the rooms of your home. It starts right from the entrance to the apartment: what catches your eye as soon as you cross the threshold? Having ten thousand sets of keys hanging from those who know which cellar or bike lock ever existed is ultimately more deleterious than having one, the right one. Clean up! Put order! You will see that you will feel better.

   Perhaps all the objects we have to give us a sense of protection. Relaxing, getting to know each other, and knowing what you want or like is a very good defense against subliminal, twisted and ambiguous messages coming from the outside.

   Go to the kitchen and open the drawers, how much delirium do you find in there? How many tea filters are there in there? But then, do you really like tea? Proceeding with the order, calm, willpower, and declutter in the bathroom, bedroom, closet, living room, and kitchen. Give a new breath of air to your space.

4. **Regularly reduce the number of objects**

   You don't have to do everything right away, give yourself weekly deadlines. Similarly, regularly reducing the objects around you by taking and throwing everything in a box without making a meaningful sorting on an emotional level will not help you.

What Is Sustainable Minimalism?

Don't make a compulsive blank slate, really think about what gratifies you and what doesn't. Maybe the dirty sock you found next to the dumpster on a crazy night means something to you, just hold on to that sock. Don't send everything to hell, but for every old and new item, think about it. Thanks to the rapid evolution of technology, nowadays just a few objects are enough to be functional in all respects.

5. **The 6-month rule**

   If you find that you have difficulty getting rid of something that you regularly propose or repurchase uselessly once a month without ever feeling satisfied with either the old or the new, allow yourself to make a choice here too. Take every single item, item, or other and ask yourself how long have I not used this thing? But how long have I not opened this magazine here? If you haven't seen certain things for more than six months, maybe it's because they don't have too much meaning for your life throw them away, give them away, tear them up, give them away, and get rid of them!

The same with relationships or dating, maybe going to have a certain experience once every forty-five days is fundamental for you and if that experience is a ritual for you, persist and keep it tight, because it is yours. Everyone needs their fixed points, just identify them!

6. **Disassociate yourself from your material possessions**

   Be careful though, you don't have to coercively deprive yourself of anything. Detaching yourself from your material possessions is also regaining possession of them. To move away and look from afar is to recognize yourself again with a clearer and more lucid eye. Do not get carried away by the trend of the moment, leave the latest new technological devices to others, leave the best-selling perfumes to others if you realize that you can do without them. Less is more precisely because that less is your very personal essential which you cannot and above all do not want to do without.

7. **It costs more to keep things than to give them away**

   Indeed, it costs more to have too much than just right! Like thoughts that distract you from what you are doing, the supernumerary of objects can also confuse you.

   Accumulating is an almost instant process nowadays, but you still try with a little effort to walk away from it! And above all, how much effort does it take to live with ten thousand visual stimuli?

   Pause to think about how much more tiring it is to be surrounded by many impulses, rather than one, clear and substantial. Dealing with an experience and a life in a minimalist way involves becoming aware of that given experience.

What Is Sustainable Minimalism?

So, if those ten thousand business cards there are only two that remind you of the company and the moment and the feeling with which you lived that lunch or that dinner, leave only those two hanging on the board. Throw the others, tear them up.

Enjoy those two memories to the full and realize how much more fulfilling a single beautiful moment is, rather than confusing your head with a thousand fleeting encounters and a thousand different sensations! Emotional or material overload costs more and more.

8. **The 20/20 rule**

There is a nice and simple way that some minimalists have thought of to help you recognize what is a symptom of impulsiveness and what is not, if the taking of an object takes you less than twenty minutes and less than twenty euros, surely it is a thing you can do without.

The decisions that require hours of reflection are the important ones, if you only spend two minutes on a question it is easy for you to care little about that question. So, for objects or new experiences, try to apply this method to calibrate their importance.

A one euro t-shirt at the market is very easy to buy, but is it why? Imagine the total expense saved minus all those single euros invested in the market every Saturday morning. Imagine how much better you can sleep when your day has been lived according to your gratifications.

9. **Quality vs quantity, look for high-quality things**

Quality must be your new paradigm. How many of those t-shirts hoarded from years of stalls did you end up wearing? Not to mention all the encounters with people who aren't important to you. Remember well that relationship quality is also fundamental.

It doesn't matter to hold on to many objects and many people, it matters to hold on to the things that matter to you. Not surprisingly, it is better to invest a lot and consciously in a single thing than casually in a varied number of objects. Do you need and want a t-shirt? Identify which one you want, spend even fifty euros and all afternoon to find it, but make sure for example that it is good and lasting. Choose the people you like to spend time with.

10. **Think before you make and buy new things**

Always ask yourself why you are making a purchase or an experience before starting, but seriously I'm about to get other pants that, oh well, almost fit me, so I only leave five euros at the most, then I throw it away? Leave it there! At most then I give it or at most I use it in that given circumstance are excuses that you can happily do without.

But do I want to spend three hours at the table with friend X this Wednesday evening too, who complains to me about the other friend Y for hours, when maybe I have other things to do? Realize that you just want to do something else and that's okay! Don't weigh yourself down if you don't feel like it, don't feel guilty about rearranging your relationships too.

11. **Dress on less**

The wardrobe, for many, can be the most hellish place in this case, and fortunately, Courtney Carver has thought of Project 333 for those who are interested in approaching minimalism.

The Project 333 is a program to follow to be minimalist right from your wardrobe, choose thirty-three items to wear for the next three months and seal the rest in a box. But be careful, in those thirty-three garments are included rings, necklaces, sunglasses, but also shoes and gym suit, outfits for the evening if something breaks or deteriorates, you can replace it, nothing extreme.

Indeed, the program helps to regain possession of one's things, the intimate and important ones. Having thirty-three garments implies having chosen them with care and respect for yourself. Above all, once chosen, it also implies the lightness of no longer having to face that decision every morning before facing the day. Free yourself from the heaviness of always having to be on top: did you choose a shirt or tank top x rather than y? That's okay, don't worry about it anymore. Donate all your one euro t-shirts, clean up everything and happily feel lighter.

12. Be grateful for what you have

When you have cleaned the apartment of various objects, when you have avoided those other three hundred t-shirts for one euro of the market, when you have also managed to re-evaluate your relationships, you will feel that wonderful sensation of unique and rare lightness that only a few things can give you.

Living well and serenely with your Less is living peacefully with yourself, it is accepting yourself. At the end of this speech, why choose minimalism then? Wanting to adopt minimalism as a lifestyle is a very intimate choice that puts you in front of many difficulties and impasses. It is not trivial, but when you have been able to reach the end of your journey, you will realize how many steps forward you have made towards self-respect.

Focus on Important Goals: most people generally have a large number of goals they want to achieve. A minimalist life has a clear purpose. To do this, you need to discover the few things that interest you most and dedicate yourself to them.

Taking care of body and mind: health is the starting point for feeling good. Therefore, it is essential to take care of yourself on two levels; the physical and the mental. Physical activity, nutrition, and sleep are the three key elements in this regard.

Cultivate Full Attention: Minimalist life requires a quiet mind and that means being free from contradictory thoughts and in tune with the present moment. Practicing mindfulness or meditation for full attention helps to recover a peaceful state of consciousness. You will be able to observe your thoughts and feelings without judging them, resisting them, feeding them, and consciously responding to situations, instead of overreacting or being exhausted by them.

CHAPTER 2

MINIMALISM: THE FIRST STEP TOWARDS A SUSTAINABLE LIFESTYLE

If you've just embarked on your journey towards a sustainable lifestyle, minimalism is a fundamental concept that will be of great help to you. Minimalism is a lifestyle that consists in eliminating the superfluous from our life, making room for the things that are important to us, surrounding ourselves only with what adds value, and improving it.

Today we live in a consumer society that bombards us with advertising, with the false promise that the latest news will improve and simplify our lives. Has it ever occurred to you that having your new cellphone, purse, or anything else would improve your life? Then, once you get it, maybe it no longer satisfies you, or you have been but for a short time, then the very latest version of the same product made you feel "backward".

Very often, we realize that we were happier when we didn't have that thing, but we wanted it, rather than when we got it. Furthermore, this mechanism leads us inexorably to find ourselves with a house full of objects that, over time, are not so useful, nor do they add value to our life. Indeed, they often end up causing us anxiety for two reasons:

1. They increase the disorder in the house

2. They make us emotionally attached to them. Sometimes for us, the loss of an object could mean losing the person or the memory connected to it.

Minimalism teaches that we don't need objects to remind us of things. This is not always the case, it happens to everyone, to find something that brings to mind beautiful moments that we didn't even think we remembered anymore. The point is precisely this, we must not eliminate everything indiscriminately. We must ask ourselves what value a certain thing has for us, and decide based on this to keep it or let it go.

Simplify our life

This concept does not extend only to things, people, daily commitments, etc. Having a sustainable lifestyle, in practice, means living your life with respect for the environment. So make choices that always take into consideration the environmental impact of what we do.

In general, it is a question of trying to reduce waste, recycle waste and use natural and sustainable products, that is, obtained through the respectful and conscious use of the resources that nature offers us. Ask yourself questions about the product from the composition to the production process.

Sustainability and minimalism could seem disconnected the two concepts, because:

- ✓ Minimalism focuses more on quantity
- ✓ Sustainability is more about quality

In the first case, a person focuses on having fewer things, which may not even be connected. In the second case, a person can own many objects, but ecological.

These two concepts have a conception because a minimalist person surrounds himself with few things but of value. So he invests in durable objects that he knows he can reuse for a long time, without having to constantly buy them back.

A person who leads a sustainable lifestyle knows that every object has a cost and an environmental impact. Therefore, it tends to buy natural, quality, reusable and long-lasting products, precisely to reduce its impact on the environment, avoiding unnecessary or disposable things. So it is clear that in reality, the two concepts are more connected than they seem. Thanks to minimalism we learn to give the right value to things. We choose higher quality items that truly bring an improvement to our life.

So, the first thing you should ask yourself before buying something is if you need it. And if that product will add value to your life and be useful to you. Once you understand this, then you can make sure that that object is also sustainable.

A lifestyle is accompanied by a zero-waste philosophy, having been born in response to consumerism and the tendency to spend on superfluous goods, filling one's street with useless things. According to Joshua Baker, minimalism is all about owning fewer things and intentionally living only with what we need, that meets our needs.

Minimalism is a clear and intentional lifestyle choice and means:

- ✓ Eliminate the distraction of the things we own in excess so that we can focus more on the things that matter most.
- ✓ Promote the things we care about most and remove anything that distracts us from them.

By promoting a simple lifestyle, minimalism bucks the mainstream culture. In addition, minimalism frees us;

- ✓ From consumerism.
- ✓ From waste and helps us reduce our environmental impact.

Minimalism and zero waste lifestyle are closely related. Living according to a zero-waste philosophy means consuming less and consuming only what we need. When we choose to be minimalist, we go in the direction of a zero-waste lifestyle because we decide to reduce consumption.

Reducing consumption is in line with two of the fundamental principles of zero waste concerning waste prevention, refuse ("refuse what we don't need") and reduce ("reduce what we need and what we cannot refuse").

4 steps to start a minimalist life

Being minimalist does not mean having less than a few personal items, wearing only black and white, and living with little. Conversely, being minimalist means living intentionally according to your personal and individual needs.

1. **Refuse the things we don't need**

    If you want to adopt a minimalist lifestyle, you must first take a step back to reconsider what you need. For example, wondering if you need to buy that new pair of shoes. In this direction, a useful exercise is, for example, not to buy something you want for at least 30 days. After 30 days, one will be able to rationally evaluate whether we need that thing or not.

2. **Decluttering the things we don't need**

   Doing decluttering, that is, rearranging the house to eliminate clutter and help free the mind from the material things that distract us and waste time. With a view to zero waste, decluttering must be done following this guide:

   i. Do not be in a hurry
   ii. Keep items you aren't sure about for a few months in a box.
   iii. Donating items that are in good condition and that we no longer use.
   iv. Recycle what can be recycled.
   v. Throw away in the undifferentiated as little as possible.
   vi. If you need to buy something, focus on the quality and sustainability of the product
   vii. To reduce waste, it is essential to purchasing items and clothing that are sustainable and of good quality (the two usually go hand in hand). This may mean spending a little more but also buying less over the distance because quality things last longer.
   viii. Give more importance to new experiences than material things.
   ix. Minimalism consists in eliminating the superfluous so that we can dedicate time to experiences that make us satisfied such as reading a book, exploring a new area of our city, planning a trip, taking a walk in the park).

CHAPTER 3

THE DIDEROT EFFECT: WHY WE BUY OBJECTS WE DON'T NEED

Diderot's scarlet dressing gown. Experts in the field of marketing and sales are looking for new ways to get us to buy goods. What we need to ask ourselves is whether we need it. How many times has it happened that you strongly desire a new item of clothing, an accessory, or simply something new? Here is what the Diderot effect explains; the tendency to consume too much is caused mainly by a natural need to own something new.

The Diderot effect takes its name from the well-known French Enlightenment philosopher Denis Diderot, who together with his colleague Jean - Baptiste d'Alembert published the Encyclopedie, what is considered the first modern encyclopedia. Diderot lived his life in poverty, but at the end of the eighteenth century, something happened that shook him. One day he bought a new dressing gown and was immediately fascinated by its beauty, he owned a soft and precious dressing gown. He quickly got rid of the old one and soon realized that this new dressing gown clashed with the rest of his possessions, which were not as good as the dressing gown. He then decided to replace most of the furnishings, choosing more and more new objects and filling the gaps that were created in the space. Soon a vicious circle was created that led Diderot to go into debt.

The Diderot Effect: Why We Buy Objects We Don't Need

The story of Diderot's dressing gown, of which the philosopher only later understood the effect it had brought in his own life, might seem ridiculous. Today, however, we behave the same way without realizing it. For example, we change the dining room table and then we want to change the chairs too, to match them with the new material. Then we feel the need to buy a new chandelier and maybe some flower pots to fill the new bigger table. Perhaps unconsciously, we are all touched by the strange effect studied by Diderot.

Diderot effect: the term coined in the twentieth century by Grant McCracken

The term Diderot effect arose only in the twentieth century when the phenomenon was better described and studied by the sociologist Grant McCracken. According to McCracken, consumers tend to buy goods following a logic consistent with their style but also following a more compulsive impulse. It is at this moment that we enter the vortex described by the term " Diderot effect ".

This mechanism arises because all consumers are driven, often unconsciously, to attribute a symbolic value to objects. This value is then exploited by marketers, who push us to buy other items that we often don't need. The Diderot effect, therefore, seems to work precisely because we are the ones who give value to objects.

The Diderot effect shows just how despite several centuries had passed, obtaining a new possession creates a spiral of consumption that leads us to always buy something new. For this reason, in the end, we buy goods that we would never have needed before. Naturally, there will always be things that necessarily have to be bought, but it is possible to put some

The Diderot Effect: Why We Buy Objects We Don't Need

techniques to focus only on what matters. If the human being enters the vortex almost unconsciously, he can defend himself, however, with small measures to no longer be a victim of the Diderot effect.

The first solution to counteract the Diderot effect is to minimize exposure: the idea is to unsubscribe from all commercial sites that offer endless catalogs of products. Then, it is necessary to get used to buying objects that fit our current style. For example; when buying new clothes, a good tactic is not to change the style, but to buy clothes that can be easily matched with the ones you already own. Learning to set limits is another fundamental practice; for example, go a whole month without buying something new. Finally, make peace with the desire for new objects: there will never be a level where people stop wanting, so accept that desire is an option provided by the mind, but not an order to follow.

CHAPTER 4
BECOMING AWARE CONSUMERS

It is becoming easier and easier to access products and services; in light of this, it is more important than ever to become aware consumers.

Conscious consumers: how do you become?

We are surrounded by products, services, and information, too many and unfiltered. Many companies, and all interested in offering us the product we cannot do without. Brilliant minds that devote all their energy to understanding how to create or strengthen needs and desires. In this scenario, it is more important than ever to be aware of consumers.

Conscious consumption has to do with the purchase of products or services that take sustainability into account. It means being able to choose responsibly and consciously the impact produced on the environment. Ultimately, this means choosing with respect for others, for oneself, and the environment.

Conscious consumers breaking down the barrier of immediate satisfaction

Conscious consumption invites us not to ignore the impact caused on nature and other living beings. It also stimulates reflection on how we invest our resources.

The environment must be taken into consideration and not just the satisfaction of an immediate need. The question we should ask ourselves is, how can I make my contribution to reducing environmental degradation? It is necessary to choose less destructive alternatives that favor collective well-being.

As consumers, therefore, we should acquire a perspective of awareness and responsibility in purchases and at home. For this, we try to offer you some simple ideas to become more eco-friendly citizens. The word "responsible" could give a feeling of heaviness, duty, and fatigue. Instead, it gives me a sense of freedom, empathy, and collectivity. Being responsible consumers, or "critical consumers", is a free choice, dictated by profound values and the desire to respect and protect our planet. Don't you think it's wonderful?

Let's start with the definition of responsible consumer, which is divided into two parts;

Consumer: the one who "consumes" goods or products from the economic system (called the market).

Responsible: someone who is responsible for their actions and behavior, suffering the consequences.

The two terms used together form the concept of responsible consumer, that is the one who buys a good or service not only based on the quality and price but also based on the environmental impact of that good or service.

But how do you become a responsible consumer?

The responsible consumer is the one who has a critical mentality on the quality and ethics of what he buys. He also has a keen sensitivity to the impact that a given product or service has on someone else. Try to find the best compromise between the buyer (himself) and the seller/producer. Sounds complicated? So let's make everything clear with the Responsible Consumer Practical Guide.

A practical guide to the responsible consumer

1. **Buy products at 0 km**

    Have you ever heard of it? The 0 km products are those that are produced and resold in the local area. They are great for several reasons.

    Support territorial and local realities

    Have fresher and more seasonal products (which have not spent days or weeks in the transport phase). They are usually cheaper (because they save on transport and, sometimes, also on the packaging). They often come to markets where it is possible to buy without using plastic bags. It is difficult to find 0 km products in supermarkets of international chains, but they are very common in markets and stalls or smaller and local grocery stores. Open your eyes and ask around and I'm sure you'll find you have some solutions right under your nose.

2. **Seasonal products are better**

The ideal responsible consumer always pays attention to buying seasonal products, because all the off-season ones are imported. That is, they come from foreign countries and very often very far away. It means that bananas all year round, or strawberries in winter, or chestnuts in spring are produced in another continent, harvested when they are still far behind in the ripening phase, spend a few weeks in the transport phase (by ship or airplane), are distributed in the various centers of the Italian territory before they reach us.

A long journey that brings with it various consequences, often the products are not very nutritious (they are harvested too early), they have a surcharge (to cover transport costs), it is not clear which substances were used for production (maybe some substance considered harmful here but who knows in Ecuador or Chile) and the lack of transparency of the producer (difficult to know the quality of life of workers, perhaps exploited or underpaid). In short, the next time you have an incredible craving for strawberries in the middle of December, think twice!

3. **Sustainable and responsible tourism**

For travel lovers or for those who can't wait for the next vacation, well even in this sector it is possible to make more responsible and careful choices. First of all, choose how to travel appropriately, you know, the plane is the fastest solution but it is also the one with the highest environmental impact. Are there any viable alternatives?

Furthermore, eco-sustainable and environmentally friendly structures should be chosen.

4. **Make Fair Trade Choices**

Fair trade products and chains are the ones that want to guarantee the respect of the worker. It is very common that they sell products from developing countries and has the aim of raising awareness of the conditions in some countries and guaranteeing the respect of their workers. They are based on direct distribution with the final consumer and go against large producers and forms of intermediation.

This is a great choice for becoming critical consumers and supporting a more ethical form of marketplace. Personally, fair trade products have often been real gems, especially as Christmas, birthday, and wedding gifts.

5. **Pay attention to energy consumption**

    Paying attention to your bill benefits not only your wallet but also the environment. Avoiding waste of consumption (such as turning off the light when not necessary) is a form of sustainability and respect

6. **Reduce waste production and recycle**

    Many believe that recycling is the solution to all evil but unfortunately this is not the case. What am I referring to? You can find the answer in my article

    It is a journey that starts from outside the walls of the house and that influences the choice of products on the supermarket shelves. Not only that, favoring certain materials (such as glass and paper) rather than others (plastic) are characteristic elements of any responsible consumer.

7. **Charity**

    Donating a portion of your profits to charity is a very noble deed.

8. **Sober lifestyle**

The responsible consumer always tries to maintain a sober lifestyle. This does not mean living a life that is poor and absent from leisure but rather choosing to marginalize waste and avoid surpluses. It is often the awareness that there is between enjoying the pleasures of life in a balanced way without harming other people or the environment. A sober lifestyle often also benefits one's health, both physical and mental, not to mention environmental ones.

CHAPTER 5
LESS PLASTIC

It is no coincidence that plastic is the major component of the vortex of garbage (called the Great Pacific Garbage Patch) which has now invaded several points of the Pacific Ocean, becoming enormous and surpassing the plankton itself in quantity. Plastic waste has invaded rivers and seas, settled on beaches and shores, and is everywhere.

Reduce plastic waste in 14 steps

1. **Discard the straws**

    One way to get plastic out of your life is to stop using plastic straws. Just ask for a glass at the bar or restaurant and decline when they offer the children the straw. Getting your children used to do without it is easy, just don't offer it to them but give them a nice cup maybe full of fruit juice!

2. **Eliminate the shopping bags**

    Use bags or recyclable bags, clean them thoroughly as food, fruit, and vegetable residues can deposit.

3. **Give up chewing gum**

Giving up chewing gum is a small thing but it will work wonders! The 'butt' is not good for you and contains plastic both inside and in the packaging.

4. **Purchase detergents in bulk**

   Again, ELIMINATE the plastic container and bring one from home to be filled with detergent 'on tap'.

5. **Buy food in bulk**

   Always prefer bulk food as well, i.e. anything you can buy without packaging. Remember that one of the expense items of the manufacturing company that recharges this cost to the buyer. YOU KNOW? Why buying in bulk is worthwhile
   - ✓ Keep the glass containers and reuse them.
   - ✓ Keep the glass, wash it and reuse it for food or other uses.
   - ✓ Reuse bottles and cups.

   It's not weird. Avoiding disposables at bars and in the office means protecting the oceans and the environment from the ever-increasing number of plastic landfills. Glass mineral water bottles are more sustainable than plastic ones. Use home water, tap water is of good quality and you can drink it!

6. **Bring your food containers**

   Shall we eat out for lunch? We get into the habit of carrying our container and asking the fast-food restaurant or restaurant where we go to put the food there. Reducing plastic waste is necessary if you care about the health of the seas

7. **Reduce the use of lighters**

   They are environmental 'killers', difficult to dispose of, they can remain unchanged even for hundreds of years. If you use them for smoking, they do double damage. If you really can't do without it, buy rechargeable: at least you will reduce waste as much as possible.

8. **Skip the frozen food counter**

   It's true, they are comfortable: you go home in the evening and dinner is ready in 5 minutes. But beware: frozen foods are the 'kings' of plastic. By buying them, you actively contribute to polluting. By trying to remove frozen foods from your diet, you will return to a healthier cuisine with natural and seasonal ingredients, of which you know the origin, and you prefer organic food.

9. **Eliminate disposable glasses, cutlery, and plates**

   Do not use disposable plates, cutlery, and glasses. They too are difficult to recycle and major polluters. Prefer the new bamboo cutlery to the classic carbon ones, they are beautiful to look at and useful.

10. **Bring the containers back to the market**

    If you buy fruit and vegetables at the market, you can bring the containers back and have them refilled. Ask your greengrocer if they take back containers, bags, and boxes to reuse.

11. **Use washable nappies**

    To produce the disposable nappies consumed by American babies every year, it takes 80,000 kg of plastic and the cutting down of more than 200,000 trees. By simply switching to cloth diapers, you can not only educate your child to respect the environment from an early age and save money.

12. **Say 'No' to fruit juices**

They often come in PET bottles and are as difficult to dispose of as or worse than a water bottle. To fruit juice, prefer a fresh fruit smoothie, you will get more antioxidants.

13. **Don't buy unnecessary detergents**

    For marketing reasons, the manufacturers differentiate detergents (floor washing, tile cleaner, countertop detergent), but this makes us spend more without counting the clutter of bottles and drums inside the house. By using vinegar and baking soda with the numerous self-made recipes, you can save money, save space and not use those harmful plastic bottles that are bad for the environment.

14. **No plastic on food**

    Avoid pre-packaged snacks and snacks, use reusable bags, plates, and containers, of the resealable type, to take the children's snacks, fruit, or lunch with you to the office. You will thus avoid packaging the food. Try just 1 of these tips, and you will have significant cash savings and also do the planet a great service.

CHAPTER 6
THE CARBON FOOTPRINT

We live in a world that is increasingly aware of climate change and the negative consequences that the carbon footprint causes to man and the environment.

The carbon footprint

The carbon footprint indicates the number of greenhouse gases generated during the production of a product or service. Accounting begins with the procurement and treatment of raw materials, then continues with the processing and production of the product, transport, use, and, finally, the disposal of the product.

Even the activities we carry out daily, such as the use of electricity from polluting energies or the use of non-electric means of transport, increase the presence of these gases and raise the average temperature of the planet leading to the catastrophic scenario of climate change. From this derive environmental disasters such as earthquakes, sea-level rise, the disappearance of species, thaw, etc.

Start reducing your carbon footprint

Currently, the carbon footprint is around 50% of the entire ecological footprint which shows how essential the reduction of this metric is to put an end to the overexploitation of resources. We must act responsibly towards our consumption.

How to calculate the Carbon Footprint

Calculating your carbon footprint is simple. It is necessary to know the number of greenhouse gases that a given activity produces and the duration in time of this activity, or the distance, in the case of transport. By multiplying the number of greenhouse gases emitted in a given time interval by the time of activity, the carbon footprint is obtained.

Let's apply the calculation to a common activity like driving a car. A diesel car produces on average 2.65 kg of CO_2 for every liter of fuel burned. In the case of a petrol car, approximately 2.37 kg of CO_2 can be produced per liter of fuel. Let's say the two cars travel 100 km. The average diesel car consumes around 7.5 liters of fuel per 100 km, while the petrol car consumes around 8.3 liters. Over a 100km journey, the diesel car produces 19.87kg of CO_2. On the same journey, the petrol car produces 19.61 kg of CO_2.

Considering these two cases, the difference is minimal. However, if we include electric cars in our calculation, the picture changes. Indeed, electric cars consume an average of 5 kWh of electricity per 100 km. This equates to 5.8 kg of CO_2 over a 100 km journey, almost a quarter of the emissions from diesel or petrol cars. Even with these activities, we generate carbon daily footprint;

- The home: the more energy we use inside our homes, the greater the carbon footprint will be.
- Air travel: the class of flight, the number of stopovers, and the number of trips are three factors that affect CO_2 emissions.

- Traveling by motorbike

Purchases, also known as secondary Footprint, include all the expense amounts incurred for a series of product categories. Expenses include TV fees, hotel and restaurant reservations, recreational and sports activities, and insurance. To the carbon footprint generated by individuals, we must also add the calculation of the carbon footprint created by the product and by an organization. Let's see them below!

Calculation of the carbon footprint generated by the product. The calculation of the product's carbon footprint includes all greenhouse gas emissions over the entire life cycle of the product. The starting point is therefore the extraction of raw materials up to final disposal. The calculation of the carbon footprint can be done by including all phases of the product life cycle, or by considering only some of them.

Product life cycle phases

Carbon footprint is calculated in compliance with the requirements contained in the technical specification known as PAS 2050. The unique international standard reference is also the ISO / TS 14067 technical specification.

Thanks to these two nomenclatures it is possible to quantify the CO_2 emissions of a product or service. The carbon footprint of a product, also known as the carbon footprint of products (CFP), is defined as the sum of the total CO_2 emissions and removals of the system that generates an asset.

Calculation of the carbon footprint generated by an organization

The organization's carbon footprint (CFO) is the quantification of greenhouse gases associated with a company. Emissions can be direct or indirect:

- ✓ Direct emissions are those coming from the company's sources or those controlled by the company itself.
- ✓ Indirect emissions are a consequence of the organization's activities, but the source of which is controlled by other companies.

The international standards for calculating this carbon footprint are the GHG Protocol and UNI EN ISO 14064-1. Both regulations provide for the obligation to consider direct and indirect emissions generated by the production of electricity and heat. We can all reduce our carbon footprint by managing and changing our consumption habits, such as;

- ✓ Use renewable energy sources: solar energy, for example, is clean and renewable energy. Furthermore, the pollution generated by the manufacturing process of solar panels is minimal and is also compensated for by the high recycling rate of these devices.
- ✓ Choose electric means of transport: As we saw in our example, an electric or hybrid car pollutes much less than a diesel or petrol car. Currently, charging stations for electric cars are very easily found in large cities, usually in parking lots or under photovoltaic shelters, which allow cars to be easily recharged. Furthermore, making sustainable mobility choices, such as using public

transport instead of private ones or renting electric scooters, helps to protect the environment.
- ✓ Contribute to reforestation: A tree can absorb 40 kg of CO_2 per year.
- ✓ Use low-energy light bulbs to save on your electricity bill too.
- ✓ Do not leave your electronic devices connected to the power for a long time.
- ✓ Be aware of the appliances that consume the most energy (e.g. hair dryer, conditioner, etc.) and buy them of the latest generation.
- ✓ Reduce your consumption of meat: Animal farms are very polluting because they consume a lot of water and increase CO_2 emissions.
- ✓ Reducing CO_2 emissions is an individual choice of environmental responsibility. We must choose sustainability in every action we take every day, such as, for example, the production of clean energy for our homes.
- ✓ Use cloth bags for grocery shopping.
- ✓ When shopping, bring your cloth bag. Plastic and its production increase the carbon footprint
- ✓ Choose class A ++: Be aware of the household appliances that consume the most energy (e.g. hair dryer, conditioner, etc.) and buy them of the latest generation.
- ✓ Do the separate collection: separating and recycling waste is important! In this way, he can receive a second life.
- ✓ Develop your creativity: give new life to old objects, indulge in modernizing them, and give them new uses.

CHAPTER 7
DIFFERENCE BETWEEN SUSTAINABILITY AND MINIMALISM

Similar in appearance but with different values, despite everything great friends. It is good to know the basics to appreciate its character and to understand its complementarity minimalism and sustainability have a lot in common but they are not the same thing.

- ✓ Both are against consumerism for different reasons.
- ✓ Both seek a "superior well-being", one more focused on the person and the other on the environment.
- ✓ Both value quality, but only one focuses more on quantity.
- ✓ Yet you can be both, one does not exclude the other. You can be minimalist, sustainable, or minimalist-sustainable.

But let's start with the basics;

Minimalism means living with the minimum. Disclaimer: I did not say "live with less" but, rather, live with the minimum. We must dispel the myth that living in a minimalist way means having a lower quality of life. Nothing more wrong! Minimalism aims for something else such as; higher quality of life, based on a key concept that we all know but few have internalized. I'm talking about the concept that "to live well it takes very little".

You don't need a thousand shoes or bags, or the most expensive car, or the most distant vacation. It doesn't take much to be happy, as long as it is intentional.

Here, the notion of "living intentionally" is one of the foundations of minimalism. I find it very fascinating. Living with "intention" means living "actively". In contrast to the passive life, where decisions, actions, and life, in general, are subjected to. The intention is the awareness of one's decisions and the commitment to achieve one's goals.

That's why being minimalist often "doesn't happen" but is instead a clear and defined intention. I like to think that minimalism only focuses on the essential, leaving everything else out. The antagonist of social pressures, he listens to only one thing: himself.

He surrounds himself with only two things:

- ✓ What is needed (food, a bed ....)
- ✓ What brings value and, therefore, a little happiness (a souvenir photo, a symbolic object ...)

Minimalism is pure simplicity. It is made up of space, air, neutrality, and silence.

What is sustainability?

Sustainability is similar but different. In common minimalism and sustainability they have an aversion to consumerism (especially unsustainable ones, such as fast-fashion) but with more scope for customization. Sustainability is also simple, but it can be colorful and confusing. You can be sustainable if you buy a lot of eco-friendly things, but you are not a minimalist. Sustainability favors a humble lifestyle, yes, but without stakes.

In the end, what matters is only one thing, is to love and respect the environment. Finding a balance with the Whole. I am aware that sustainability also means reducing one's environmental impact, and that to do this it is necessary to buy and have less. Unlike minimalism, however, sustainability leaves room for choice: buy less if you want, otherwise buy better (for example, buy used or fair trade).

A responsible consumer takes responsibility for the consequences of his actions, trying to reduce the negative effects to a minimum. A sustainable life takes responsibility for the well-being of the environment and the community, near and far. Unlike minimalism, which has no responsibility towards others, except that of living according to its principles. Ultimately, the core of a sustainable lifestyle is based on a few simple concepts, live responsibly or live without harming anyone or anything live in a balanced way with the environment and with other people live in a conscious way of one's actions and consumption.

Minimalism: it focuses on a few things but without necessarily taking care of the origin

Sustainability: allows you to own many (but not too many) things of sustainable origin (which does not harm other people or the environment)

Sustainable Minimalism: it values the quality and origin of the few things it surrounds itself with

Responsible Consumer: the one who buys also considering the environmental and social impact of this good or service

Consumerism: an attitude of indiscriminate purchase of consumer goods, especially non-primary and unnecessary goods.

CHAPTER 8
THE DECLUTTERING

Have you ever felt suffocated in the house due to all the objects in every room that create disorder? Do not worry, it is a sensation common to many homes that are often excessively full of objects that risk-taking over and creates chaos that can generate a feeling of discomfort and throw you into despair.

What to do?

The secret is to eliminate, in a conscious and reasoned way, all that we have accumulated over time and which is useless or does not represent something necessary or important for us. The way you organize your space can therefore affect, both positively and negatively, your state of mind and your mood. A tidy and organized home makes us feel better, at peace with ourselves, and decluttering can help.

What is decluttering?

It is therefore the ability to make room and get rid of the superfluous.

It is a very powerful weapon to improve your life, to make you master your space and time again: by learning to get rid of the superfluous, you will immediately feel better and in a good mood. Here are 5 simple steps to eliminate the superfluous from your home

1. **Things to know before you begin**

Decluttering requires a good dose of decision and the ability to live with small moments of melancholy and nostalgia. While you make room and get rid of the superfluous, you dive into the past. So decluttering becomes a way to also do inner cleansing.

Don't be in a hurry to do everything right away, but proceed step by step so that you can choose whether to dedicate half an hour a day to decluttering or to do everything over the weekend.

Don't move deleted things to the attic or basement for decluttering to make sense, the things you don't need must be eliminated. The decluttering process should not be seen as deprivation but as a fun and creative journey towards a regained simplicity.

2. How to recognize a superfluous object?

This is the focal point of the whole process. The first few times it may seem difficult, but slowly you will be able to recognize superfluous objects on the fly. Look at each item in the room you are tidying up, and ask yourself:

I. If you still like it.
II. If it is useful.
III. If it has sentimental value.

Any item that does not meet one of these three criteria must be put aside. Do not keep an object just because your mother gave it to you and you think she would be upset if she didn't see it anymore or because "one day" it might come in handy; if you haven't used it so far, it means that you can make use of it, unless forever.

Decluttering means just getting rid of the superfluous and tidying up. The idea of living a simpler life with fewer material things interests many, but they often find themselves not knowing where to start and asking themselves many questions, such as:

"What if I still need this object?" As we said before, if you haven't used it until now, you can do without it. "Isn't it bad to throw away things that still work?". You don't have to throw them away, you can give them away, sell them or donate them to charity, but more on that later.

The wardrobe is the perfect example; how many useless clothes do we tend to accumulate without realizing it? How many clothes do we wear? Take it all out, choose and then decide what to donate and what to throw away.

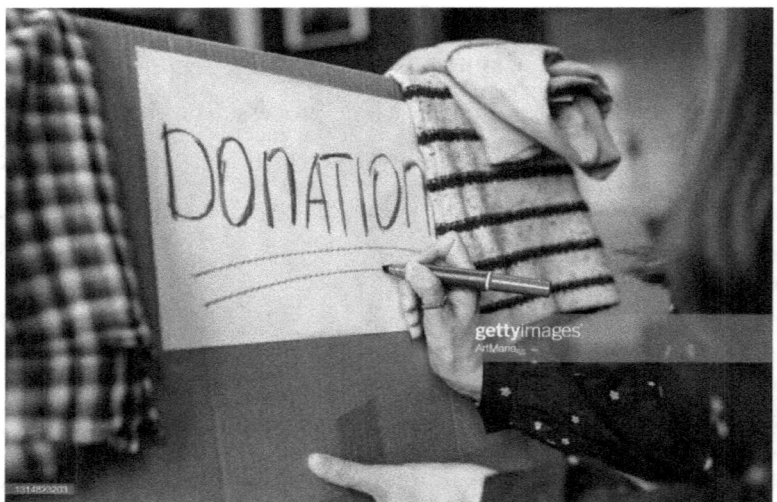

Some shops take old clothes back in exchange for shopping vouchers.

Here are some examples of items to delete;

- ✓ Dry cleaners hangers
- ✓ Sports gadgets
- ✓ Tablecloths too large or small

The Decluttering

- ✓ Mismatched socks
- ✓ Unnecessary business cards
- ✓ Souvenirs you don't like
- ✓ Stained, torn, or frayed towels
- ✓ Outdated video games
- ✓ Notebooks that are no longer needed
- ✓ Store catalogs available online
- ✓ Ruined clothes
- ✓ Broken electronic appliances
- ✓ Cookbooks you've never used
- ✓ Shoes that hurt, old, or worn out
- ✓ Broken toys or board games with missing pieces
- ✓ Dishes you never use
- ✓ Greeting cards, wedding invitations, etc.
- ✓ Old calendars
- ✓ Empty shoeboxes
- ✓ Boxes of electronic devices whose warranty has expired
- ✓ chargers and old cables of various types
- ✓ Unused or damaged backpacks and bags
- ✓ Decorative elements (favors) that you no longer like
- ✓ Cosmetics that are out of date or you don't like and nail polishes that have congealed
- ✓ Damaged or unworn jewelry (e.g. mismatched earrings, broken necklaces)
- ✓ And here's why you won't miss these things:
- ✓ They are old: you will never wonder why you have thrown away all those unused cables or those uncomfortable shoes.

- ✓ They're broken if you wanted to fix those things, you would have already done so.
- ✓ You and your family no longer need them; don't forget, if you needed them you would use them.

3. How to organize the decluttering

There are two paths you can take, depending on how you are best at the organizational level:

1st method: go to rooms.

2nd method: go for types of products.

Go for rooms

It is the simplest system to follow because it allows you to work on something targeted: just choose the room to arrange and work on it until you have obtained the desired result.

How to organize the work?

Take out everything you want to analyze (for example all the clothes in the closet) and place it on a free surface. Divide all the items by choosing whether to keep them, throw them away, or give them away.

Make a thorough cleaning of the spaces, and store the objects to keep organizing them as you think best suited to your needs.

It is essential to put away everything that is used regularly and instead put in the most uncomfortable places what is used occasionally. Using suitable quality boxes and baskets will help to keep things clean and tidy more easily and to put things away quickly once used. Finally, it is very useful to use labels when storing something that is rarely used.

To simplify the process, you can divide it into two stages. Sure you'll be sure you want to delete some items, but you may have some doubts about others. Then put all the objects in "maybe" in a box or bag; after the first elimination you will have a clearer idea about the usefulness of keeping something of what you have temporarily placed in the box and you will be able to act accordingly. Proceed in this way room by room, until you have completed the whole house.

A little trick: to keep your clothes tidy, buy some fabric boxes (you can buy them from Ikea or online) and put away the clothes. If you roll them up, when you take them out to put them on they won't have creases!

Go for types of products

It is the most complicated system since not all clothing is in the bedroom wardrobes in the house, electronic equipment is not all in the same room as well as ornaments, books, magazines, etc.

Going for products means examining the whole house by focusing on a certain product (example: electronic equipment) and acting on it. The work is certainly more complex, but in many cases, it offers better results.

Look for all the objects of a certain category and store them, if you can, all together so that you always know where they are. You can put all your phone accessories and chargers in small bins - these bins are also used to organize drawers.

Decluttering: keeping the "memories" yes or no?

Most of the objects we have at home do not serve a specific task, but are part of the "memory" of the life of one's family; I'm talking about letters, photo albums, objects dear to our ancestors, and much more. In this case, the choice is personal and must be made after careful reflection on the importance that certain memories can have in family life.

4. **What to do with the objects to be eliminated?**

Donating to Associations: I always recommend donating as much as possible to local charities and organizations. Donating what you don't need is twice as good: you'll have fewer things taking up space in your home, and other people get items they need.

Give to someone you know: maybe relatives or friends need something that you own and no longer use but it is in good condition, give it to them: from clothes put on once and never again to equipment for children (seats, cots, etc.), anything that can help them will be seen as a very welcome gift.

Resell: if you have any valuables you don't use (jewelry, appliances, silverware, etc.) you can always resell them online or in thrift markets. In case you want to get rid of antique furniture, call an antique dealer for an appraisal so you know their exact price.

Throw away: Finally, don't feel guilty if a lot of things, especially if broken, end up in the trash. Always remember: your home is not a warehouse. Some things must be thrown away, adopting the most appropriate system from time to time; undifferentiated or differentiated garbage for small and medium-sized objects, while landfill for larger objects and household appliances. Remember to respect the environment!

Special Mention: The Decluttering of Books

A necessary premise: books should never be thrown away, for any reason in the world. So, if you need to make room in the library or your house is too crowded with books, the keyword is given as a gift.

If you have accumulated too many books, you could try donating them or you can simply give them away to your friends and family. Among the possible recipients of the books, you have discarded are neighborhood libraries, schools, hospitals, retirement homes, prisons, and other types of communities.

5. **The trick of the bag**

   To keep the house tidy after fixing it or before, to make an initial roughing;

   ✓ Get a bag.
   ✓ Decide what to focus on (Paper? Plastic? Other?).
   ✓ Take a tour of the whole house.

Throw everything that is too much into the bag, without thinking about it so much. Fill the bag as fast as you can. When it is full, do not put it on hold get out of the house immediately and throw everything away. How do you feel?

Do you feel a feeling of relief and lightness? The secret of the success of this system is zero organization.

✓ It's so simple it can't fail.
✓ It is perfect for giving a first "blow" to an overcrowded house.
✓ It gives a feeling of relief and success instantly and with little effort.
✓ It is very effective as a maintenance technique.
✓ It can be applied in the vast majority of situations.

The technique has its limits, it cannot take you alone to "solve" an entire house but to do skimming and to start a decluttering that seems stuck to the starting grids, the bag trick is ideal. What do you think about it? Try to make sure you go by material: use a plastic bag for all plastic objects, a paper bag for sheets and documents, and so on, to simplify the recycling of materials.

Finally a tidy and livable house

When the job is done you will have the surprise of discovering a more spacious house, where everything has its place and there are no piles of unused objects.

How to keep the results over time?

Make purchases aware that they are not going to fill your home with superfluous items again. To adopt this little rule for everything that enters one must go out. Use the bag trick frequently to avoid the new accumulation of items.

I'm sure that once this hard work is done, you will have no desire to go back to your old messy and stuffy house, the satisfaction of being surrounded only by beautiful objects that represent us will be stronger than any form of laziness. A roundup of ideas for ordering your home after throwing away the superfluous elements.

Bathroom idea

Idea 1: if you have a drawer, organize it with small boxes to divide the various products in this way everything will have its place and you will not waste time looking for things.

Idea 2: if you have doors instead of drawers, no problem. Store the products in baskets, better if made specifically for the organization then divided internally.

Wardrobe idea

Idea 1: for the drawers use dividers to find everything on the fly.

Idea 2: instead of folding sweaters and T-shirts, roll them up on themselves so as not to create creases and to optimize space.

Closet idea

Idea: To organize the closet, you can use boxes. This will facilitate not only the organization but also the change of season just swap the boxes with the clothes of the past season with the boxes of the current one.

Kitchen idea

Idea 1: to make more space, use shelves.

Idea 2: make the most of the space under the sink by using containers for bulkier products and a basket to hang on the door for smaller products.

Idea 3: even in the refrigerator, use containers to separate the various products and keep everything in order.

As we have seen, it is good to get rid of what we do not need to have more space for what makes us happy.

10 tips for tidying up

Any advice to get started?

1. If nothing is upside down in the house, everything will be fine. Yes, even on Monday morning.

The Decluttering

2. Get rid of what you don't need so that you can have more space for what makes you happy.
3. Give a second life to what you don't use. So, you are good for the planet.
4. Labels are your best friends.
5. Do not leave anything to chaos, not even the wardrobe.
6. Remember, if order reigns supreme, live like a king.
7. Keep everything you care about in plain sight. Not everything, everything.
8. Plan your way, perhaps by color.
9. Say goodnight to clutter: you will have better dreams.
10. Order everything and then reward yourself with a box. Yes, but biscuits.

CHAPTER 9
MARIE KONDO'S RULES FOR HOME DECLUTTERING

The KonMari method, invented by cleaning guru Marie Kondo has conquered the world. It all began with the publication of the best-seller "The Life-Changing Magic of Tidying Up; The Japanese Art of Decluttering and Organizing ", published in Italy with the title "The magical power of tidying up: The Japanese method that transforms your spaces and your life ".

A bestseller that has only anticipated a real revolution in the world of tidying, or rather the Netflix series "Let's tidy up with Marie Kondo ", boom! A method that promises to restore order, light, and joy in the home (and perhaps in life), through many small tricks, however, applied with particular rigor. All very interesting, but in practice where do you start?

According to the KonMari method, it is not necessary to proceed by room, but by category of objects, strictly in this order: clothes, books, papers, and Komono (or ... miscellany). Everything, therefore, belongs to a macro or sub-category and it is strongly recommended to collect all the objects belonging to the same category, arrange them on the floor, or in any case on a flat surface, which can be a bed or a table and analyze them one by one to choosing to know their fate. Before deciding what to keep and what to throw away, and before letting yourself go to the memories, ask yourself "Does it make me happy?"

This is a key point of the KonMari method you have to surround yourself with beautiful things, which remind us of happy moments and which, looking at them, make you feel joy and well-being.

So let's throw away that pair of jeans that we have been promising ourselves to wear for two years when we have lost 5 kg (making us feel inadequate in the meantime), away with those books that collect dust and we haven't opened for ten years, away with that box full of papers, ribbons, pens and objects of various kinds that have been closed for months.

Not everything should be thrown in the garbage, indeed, when possible we strongly recommend donating, giving away, or reselling what you no longer use, but in some cases, the only possible answer, unfortunately, is the garbage nerd.

Everything at once

KonMari's method is unforgiving is best to apply it all at once, even if this means taking a whole day in the intent. Postponing or dividing the method into too many phases would seem the best way to fail. If Madame Marie Kondo says so, who are we to contradict her?

Clothes

How many clothes have been sitting in the closet for months, if not years? In addition to the clothes, even those socks that have been unmatched for months, the underwear with the now gone elastics, scarves that we last put on back in 2005 everything has been put away.

Only clothes that are worn regularly in the Spring/Summer and Autumn/Winter seasons should remain in the wardrobe, while everything else must disappear. How clothes are folded and hung is also important, here are some demonstration images of the KonMari method for bringing zen joy to the closet.

Books

Even if we like full bookcases and houses overflowing with books, in fact over the years we risk accumulating a good amount of titles that we will never read again, and that only take away space, accumulating dust.

The used book market, for example, is very active, but associations, literary clubs, bookcrossing, and libraries can also be good choices to "free" the books that we no longer need.

Marie kondo's rules for home decluttering

Sheets, slips, and scattered papers

The great enemies of clutter, pop up in all corners of the house, from the desk to the bookcases from the fridge to the drawers. Old receipts, photocopies, flying notes, printed lists are all things we haven't looked at for months, but which continue to make the house and our life more messy and crowded.

In this case, no mercy, the important thing is to save the important documents, the rest must be thrown away. The miscellany is perhaps the most complicated part to fix because it encompasses everything. Everyone knows what brings disorder into their home, the important thing is to keep in mind another tip that is part of the KonMari method opines that before putting everything back in order, immediately throw away all the discarded things, avoiding accumulating them in the garage or a box.

The KonMari method recommends proceeding by rearranging the objects by category following this ladder; first the clothes then the documents followed by various objects to concentrate only at the end on the objects of emotional value or the memories, considered the most difficult to let go of.

Marie Kondo argues that we should only keep objects capable of arousing us joy and positive feelings. This will make it easier for everyone else to fit into the pile of objects to separate us from. The golden rule shouldn't be choosing what to throw away, but selecting what you want to keep.

The tidying up exercise should be constant over time. It might be useful to apply the golden rules of the decluttering guru.

These are:

- To put in order.
- Imagine and commit to pursuing the ideal lifestyle.
- Sort by category and never by location or one room at a time.
- Follow the order indicated and ask yourself for each article if it arouses joy.

- The state of mind of the people will also benefit. In this way, we will eliminate the superfluous, even objects and clothes that can arouse bad memories in us.
- A useful tip, in case of indecision, is to put objects in a box that we are not convinced we want to throw away. Taking back its contents three months later to understand that it was not

necessary to keep those objects, so we can permanently eliminate them in a convinced and conscious way.
- Among the tips that come from the Kondo tidying method, we remember the grouping of objects by categories: fabrics, paper, and electrical material.
- Other labels will be liquids, such as hygiene, cleaning and beauty products, food, and tableware.

Tidying up the cupboard

Each space containing the aforementioned objects, such as wardrobes, doors, boxes, and drawers, must be filled to 90% to make the most of the space. As for the arrangement of the wardrobe, Marie Kondo's method suggests perfectly folding clothes, including dresses, as well as t-shirts, shirts, and trousers. Only heavy fabrics, jackets, suits, and coats should be hung. We proceed with the arrangement by completely emptying the wardrobe and then start selecting, choosing what to keep and what to get rid of.

Closet decluttering

Arranging things vertically is the most effective solution for Kondo to visualize everything well. Even the accessories must be rearranged following rules: the bags placed one inside the other, the folded canvas bags and the same goes for underwear and socks.

Even for the arrangement of documents, as happened for the wardrobes, the method of emptying everything and throwing away as much as possible applies. The documents must be divided by types such as guarantees, bills, contracts, and each placed in a special container.

Furthermore, we also want to suggest the rules of another exponent of decluttering Geraline Thomas

Geraline Thomas decluttering rules

Geraline Thomas, an expert in home organization, also teaches us methodically how to organize the house, eliminate the superfluous and make room only for the necessary. For her, all the things you don't use, you don't like anymore, you don't know what to do with them and you don't want to clutter, that is, to be eliminated.

Not doing this is just an excuse

Always starting from the wardrobe, it is important to remember that each garment should spend 80% of its life on us and not hanging. If it doesn't, because it no longer fits, we have changed size or tastes. We proceed by donating it to friends or charity.

It is starting from the entrance to the house, everything we do not use at least once a week must be eliminated, it is not needed and clutters the area that should be our business card. As for Marie Kondo, also in this system, the likes must be put together with the like this is true in the bathroom, in the pantry, and the wardrobe. This way you will find everything easily.

Reorganize spaces and tidy up the house

Avoid creating spaces where articles of different kinds converge: in the mixed drawer we will never really know what to look for or find. Using better means using less and in the same way, buying fewer means using more we keep this mantra in mind every time we are about to make a purchase.

We proceed by eliminating gadgets, giveaways, and other items we have at home for no real reason. Finally, we pay attention to products to clean the house: we often accumulate bottles, we buy them in quantity in case of offers but not everything is needed and above all, it takes up space.

CHAPTER 10

HOW TO ORGANIZE YOUR CLOSET WITH THE SSO METHOD (EMPTY, SELECT AND THEN ORGANIZE)

A re you renovating your bedroom and would like to buy a new wardrobe? Would you like to size and organize your wardrobe with a precise and functional method? The wardrobes we see on the various sites are very beautiful, right? But then when we find ourselves replicating that situation in our home, we don't even see the shadow of the wardrobe we were inspired by. We want to show you all the necessary considerations to make before buying a wardrobe and all its magnificent interior accessories.

First, you need to do some decluttering, get rid of the superfluous, or identify what you need and eliminate what you no longer use. This initial skimming will help you get a more complete view of what you need and how to organize it. Only later, when it has been decided what to keep, can we move on to the organization, that is, to assign a well-defined location to each item of clothing.

Apparently, it may seem a boring and complicated operation (in fact I am honest, well done decluttering takes time and effort), but if applied with the right method and with a bit of willpower, you can get great results and enormous benefits, both physically and mentally. How cool is it to immediately find a thing when looking for it? How nice is it to know what to wear in the morning, without spending hours in front of the wardrobe?

To be honest, your closet contains a lot of things that you never put on, that no longer fit you, or that have worn out over time. What do you do with these things if you don't need them? They only take up space for nothing, space necessary to keep the garments less pressed to each other and to see them better. Thanks to this method you will understand how pleasant it will be every morning to find what you are looking for immediately, moreover, your garments will have much fewer creases than now, because they will no longer be compressed inside the wardrobe.

The SSO method: clear select and then organize

This reordering method brings together the decluttering phase with that of the organization. A method that can be applied throughout the home and for every category of objects, but in this chapter, we dedicate ourselves to the wardrobe: let's start. An easy-to-apply method that allows you to organize and make your wardrobe functional.

Empty

Empty the wardrobe and place all the clothes on the bed, I recommend not leaving anything out. This exercise is used to become aware of how many things you have and above all how many things are unused. Who knows, maybe you can also find something you thought you lost.

Select

For each item, ask yourself these questions;

- ✓ Do I use it frequently (during its season of course)?
- ✓ Do I have nothing else like it that performs its function?
- ✓ Is it in good condition and not damaged or worn?
- ✓ Is it the right size and does it enhance me?
- ✓ Does it excite me when I hold it in my hand?

If you answered yes to at least 3 out of 5 of these questions, that item is to be kept. Everything else must be eliminated (give, sell, exchange, recycle or throw away). Focus on what is to be kept and not what is to be discarded.

Do you have doubts about some items and wonder if you will still use them? Generally, if you never wore it the previous season, you probably won't wear it. If you still have doubts, put those garments in a closed box, which you will take to the basement or attic, or garage. If in the following months you do not come to look for them, then you will have the confirmation that those clothes were no longer needed and then proceed with the elimination, without any remorse. All those garments related to memories, the wedding dress or the dress of your graduation party, which for obvious reasons you will no longer wear, are put in a closed container.

Organize

After deciding what to keep, you need to arrange and organize all the clothing items in their location. Everything must be in its place. Using the bed as a support surface, divide all the items into categories:

- ✓ Clothes

- ✓ Tops and blouses
- ✓ T-shirt
- ✓ Jeans
- ✓ Trousers
- ✓ Skirts
- ✓ Sweaters
- ✓ Cardigan
- ✓ Sweatshirts
- ✓ Shirts
- ✓ Jackets
- ✓ Coats
- ✓ Blazer
- ✓ Pajamas
- ✓ Intimate
- ✓ Socks
- ✓ Shorts
- ✓ Swimwear
- ✓ Sportswear
- ✓ Shoes
- ✓ Bags
- ✓ Accessories
- ✓ Jewelry and watches

After dividing these categories, you will better understand the volumes and quantities to be organized. The next step is to understand what to hang and what to store in specific drawers or containers.

Based on what to put where you should be able to roughly identify how many drawers you need, how much hanging space, and how many other interior accessories. Grab a pen and paper and try to draw the prospect of your ideal wardrobe. Alternatively, you can also help you with the Ikea Planner, very useful for composing the wardrobe and previewing the final result.

One last tip

To further organize the hanging area of your closet keep the categories divided and keep them separated simply by a play of colors. I'll give you an example if you have to organize blouses, shirts, and blazers in a hanging module, place the darker blouses from left to right up to the lighter ones, then move on to the darker shirts up to the light ones and proceed to the same way with everything else. Now you can organize your closet and that of your children efficiently and functionally.

CHAPTER 11
20 MINIMALIST HABITS FOR A SIMPLER LIFE

Life, if you prefer, is made up of routine, of small daily gestures that follow one another. Acquiring minimalist and healthy habits improves your life considerably because it simplifies the way we live. Without realizing it, we often tend to complicate life when it is much simpler and more beautiful than what we believe. So let's see how to improve our life.

The minimalist habits that change your life

1. **Do not depend on the opinion of others**

    Simply put, you have to give a damn about what others think. How can this habit make life easier? Because doing what you want while ignoring the common thought or of other people who may not even know each other, makes you happy and satisfied with yourself without unnecessary stress. This habit changes life because as soon as you learn not to think about the opinion of others it will be possible to live an authentic life and make choices dictated by personal preferences.

2. **Having few clothes**

    How many times have you found yourself in front of the open wardrobe wondering what to put on? In reality, this is a real waste of time as well as energy. Thinking less about clothes, about buying them and how to find the best combination makes life easier. Having too many clothes means occupying not only a physical space but also a mental space. At this point, the best thing would be to acquire minimalist habits and have fewer clothes to ensure that you don't waste time and stress every day about choosing what to wear.

3. **Remain silent**

It may seem strange to say but saving on words is important. Making too many speeches to fill the void leads nowhere. Being silent from time to time and listening is instead a profitable and pleasant habit. If you adopt this habit with the simplicity you will find that people enjoy spending time with you and you can gain in mental health and relaxation.

4. **Ask yourself questions**

Often we find ourselves taking actions without thinking about what we are doing or the reasons why they are being done. It can happen, for example, when you eat out of habit and not out of true hunger, or when you are buying a dress without needing it and we like it. Stopping to ask every now and then why we perform certain gestures can significantly improve our attitude towards life. This attitude allows you to get out of habits that you do not like or that are unhealthy by simplifying your life.

5. **Choose a dress code**

To further simplify your life by acquiring minimalist habits regarding the choice of clothes to wear every day, my advice is to choose a sort of uniform and have a minimal dress code that you can interchange and therefore spend less time choosing the right clothes. to every day. The important thing is to choose clothes that are comfortable and suitable for multiple occasions, thus creating a functional wardrobe or capsule wardrobe. A capsule wardrobe means having a (limited) number of easily combinable and interchangeable clothes belonging to a color palette with which you can create a certain number of outfits.

6. **Make the to-do list**

This habit is a must to increase your productivity and clear your mind. Drawing up a to-do list the night before for the next day, or organizing a list for the coming week helps you stay organized, don't waste time and always know what to expect. The to-do list also helps you understand how many activities you can bring.

7. **Stop doing multiple things at once**

Multitasking is a skill that is always required in the workplace but is not healthy. Dedicating your mind and body to one task at a time makes it possible to pay more direct attention and focus well on one goal and accomplish one at a time. It is never really possible to focus on multiple things at once and for this reason, it is best to learn to be more selective.

8. **Start saying no**

Simplifying life and feeling good is also synonymous with having to give up something. Say no to meetings or appointments in which you have no interest, say no to collaborations or job requests, even if it means missing out on some opportunities. We must learn to prioritize the things that make us waste time.

9. **Take deep breaths**

Focusing on your breath allows you to relax, establish contact, and have a firm point with the present. Remembering to breathe means putting your feet back on the ground and being more aware. You should start taking this as a minimalist habit to do in the morning, perhaps taking three good deep breaths before starting the day.

10. **Step by step**

    Routine is something sacrosanct, it serves to understand which moments of the day to dedicate to a certain type of activity and establishes an order of things. Minimalist habits are acquired, with time and organization, and proceed step by step, without wanting everything immediately. To get started, just prioritize and focus on one thing at a time. Not only that, there we will simplify life but we will have more time for ourselves.

11. **Do not pollute the visual environment**

    Having a tidy and clean room, with the cables of the electronic devices well hidden and objects arranged in an orderly manner, allows you to live in a more relaxed way and to have an orderly, light, and peaceful mind.

12. **Decluttering thoughts**

    Every day we are exposed to a flood of constant thoughts. What minimalist habits allow us to do is to avoid harmful and futile thoughts, leaving room for what matters. It must also be done decluttering of thoughts and throwing away what is thrown away. Maybe instead of postponing a commitment, it is better to do it, and implement the theory of the famous saying "easier said than done".

13. **Always carry a bottle with you**

Drinking enough water means feeling good and thinking about your health. One of the minimalist habits that make life easier is always carrying a water bottle.

14. Practice half-yearly decluttering

A couple of times a year are enough to take stock of the situation. Letting go of useless things and objects means simplifying your way of life and knowing which things matter and which ones you can start doing without. I recommend watching the video: Decluttering wardrobe after 3 years of minimalism

15. Eliminate distractions

Between computers, smartphones, social networks, and various things, it is always easier to be prey to unnecessary distractions. A few simple gestures are enough to avoid getting distracted:

- ✓ Turn off notifications on your smartphone
- ✓ Unsubscribe from unnecessary newsletter subscriptions
- ✓ Delete intrusive applications
- ✓ Mute WhatsApp groups
- ✓ Set a timer for time to spend on social media

16. Clean rest

You have to choose to have a quality rest, perhaps without background noise, such as radio, TV, and music. Peace of mind can be achieved simply by silence.

17. Stroll

No one could have imagined this activity among the minimalist habits to be acquired to live in a simpler and better way, yet walking helps to clear the mind. It relaxes the mood and mitigates ailments. You should take a daily walk to stay active and healthy.

18. Minimalist furniture

The best moments in life are those spent with people who love each other without too many worries. Essentially furnishing your home helps you not to waste too much time on cleaning and therefore to have more time to spend as you prefer. In short, a simple house is also a panacea for daily chores.

19. No make up

In the morning, when you wake up and get ready, you waste a lot of time in the make-up phase because there are so many women who can't help but put on make-up before going out. For many people, make-up has become an addiction and not a pleasure or a will. For this reason, it is advisable to ask yourself why you wear makeup and rediscover the pleasure of not wearing makeup.

20. Don't try to fill all your time

Many tend to obsessively fill their days with activities and often can't find time for the simpler things. But now and then you also have to indulge in sweet idleness.

CHAPTER 12
HOW TO SAVE WITH MINIMALISM

Let's talk about budget and minimalism. Minimalism isn't just about cutting down on all the things you buy and letting go of the objects. You can also incorporate it into your finances. The idea is simple. We need to understand what are the superfluous things we can do without. But how does a minimalist budget work? Let's dig in and find out exactly how to incorporate a minimalist budget and minimalism into your finances.

What is a minimalist budget?

Minimalism means identifying and understanding what you value most in not just your physical assets, but your life as well. According to Joshua Becker, an author, and advocate of minimalism, minimalism is all about intentionally removing things that distract us from what matters most to us.

Anyone can have a minimalist budget. It's good for people who want to cut down on their expenses or set up a new budgeting system. If you're looking to cut back on expenses but find yourself shopping a lot, then a minimalist budget might be worth considering.

The secret to financial well-being exists. What does it mean to feel good? In general, it means having enough money to live and not having large debts on your shoulders, rather having even the little that remains to be set aside for the future or any eventuality. Saving with minimalism is a completely different approach to money and life than usual.

The minimalist lifestyle incorporates the idea that you can live with less to live better. It is a lifestyle that is not only practical and material but also a mental one. A simple and authentic life cannot be exchanged for any other false and wasteful life. Minimalism is practiced by many people, even without others noticing. It is often associated with austerity, but the intent here is precise to make it clear that minimalism is not renunciation, but rather it is a considered choice.

The basic idea to incorporate is that money makes us free to do everything, and it is important not to trade our freedom for useless objects and empty experiences. You do not have to give up a good coffee at the bar with friends, because the mere giving up as an end in itself does not lead to anything, but it worsens the situation and does not allow you to save. A bit like what happens when you fast as a punishment and then eat more than the previous day. What the minimalist attitude helps to do is improve one's relationship with money, and this results in actual savings.

The rules for saving with minimalism

There are several ways to approach the minimalist lifestyle to save;

1. **Don't buy what you can't afford**
   It sounds easy but not everyone follows this simple rule. Sometimes, being able to buy things in installments gives the impression of being able to afford many things, but buying things that you cannot afford puts you in the position of debtors, and therefore a disadvantageous position. Consequently, you will depend on your job and therefore you will make life choices

dictated by money rather than by desire or interest. Buying things that cannot be afforded limits freedom and oppresses, limits the personality, and involves life choices that do not belong to us. Can I afford what I'm buying? Could the purchase I am making affect my freedom? Asking these questions can truly change your life and save you from situations that may cause difficulties in the future.

2. **Do declutter (letting go of the superfluous)**

   Essentially, not wasting also means saving. Getting rid of unnecessary things is liberating, things that you have and that you don't need to tend to occupy not only space but also the mind. Having too many things also means worrying about your belongings and living in constant stress.

3. **Don't spend to impress**

   If you are not rich it is useless to spend as if you were rich. Don't spend money on others, to impress them, or to get social approval. Living below your means is the only real way to save, but you need to free yourself from the social pressures that may arise.

4. **Saving money with minimalism**

   When it comes to saving with minimalism, we are talking about a lifestyle, an approach to money, and a life that is completely different from the usual. It is not to be seen as renunciation or sacrifice. It is about welcoming a new philosophy that makes you fully enjoy what you have and what you can afford.

5. **Eliminate impulse buying**

It is enough simply to assume a different mental form and ask yourself; Do I need it? Do I need to drink coffee at the bar or can I do it at home? If drinking coffee out with my friend makes me feel better, then it's okay. However, there are many purchases made on the spot that does not have a positive effect on our life. Avoiding impulse purchases is a symptom of wisdom and allows, in addition to saving, to have a low impact on the environment and make a gift to future generations.

6. **Don't confuse needs with desires**

    Often the objects you see in advertisements, on billboards, and on social media, clothes worn by influencers or things they own, do nothing but fuel the public's need to own those products. The desire to be like them becomes a primary necessity. Advertising must create a need where it did not exist before. Unfortunately, more people are fascinated by false lifestyles, created specifically to confuse us and push us to buy. The advice that is always valid in these cases, given that in one way or another we are all victims of advertising, is to remain true to yourself. Knowing exactly what you want, what you need is the first step towards a more conscious life and guaranteed savings.

7. **Enjoy what you have**

    Perhaps not many people know that in reality we only use 20%8, of what we own, the rest is confusion, wasted time, and money. There are more times that one passes by desiring things that one does not have than those spent appreciating what one has instead. Now it would be enough to stop and consider this aspect of life, the one that sees us as privileged people compared to others who do not have everything, and suddenly we will be happier.

8. **Inquire about**

   This step towards awareness cannot always be done independently. Sometimes it is necessary to inquire and find support in books that can give advice, and open the mind. For this reason, reading is a valuable aid towards change and there are some interesting books regarding personal finance that can make a difference.

   If I think about how much money I have wasted in vain in recent years, I'm scared. I've been decluttering this weekend and I'm still in disbelief at the amount of stuff I have. I have so many summer dresses that I could wear a different piece every day all summer long. Of all those items, I'm sure, I will always wear the same dozen or so things.

9. **I certainly learned my lesson**

   Shopping consciously and in the right proportions helps us to set aside money that can be invested in experiences that improve our lives, or that simply make us grow, make us happy and make us feel good without having to have something material to flaunt

10. **Have more budget for experiences**

    Since I stopped filling gaps by buying random things that I didn't even take out of the bag once I got home, I realized that I had a lot more budget for travel, for courses, for cinema, exhibitions, and theater, for everything that at the end of the month it would make me feel happy with a life well spent.

11. **Work less for more**

    What if I told you that if you want less you can also afford to work less? When I bought my first home, I compromised. I would not have had it in the chicest neighborhood, I would not have had a terrace and I would have been in an apartment building. The house I chose was in an area that I knew well, with many services, and that allowed me to get to the center and to work on foot if I wanted. And while it doesn't have amazing views, it has two balconies, is exposed on both sides, and is much larger than what I could have afforded downtown.

Being essential leads to downsizing the things you need, the minimalist mindset helps you do just that. In not complicating your life.

Having material assets to manage is exhausting. Having a car means taking care of it, investing in insurance, expenses, costs of various kinds that are practically constant. I have a car, I bought it used after they stole the first one I had received as a graduation gift from my parents, a Yaris, and even used I always chose one of the same models. Ditto for a large house that has more space than what we need. One step at a time but you can make a lot of difference.

12. I want to save money!

These are simple tricks with which you will be able to easily save hundreds or thousands of euros every year, according to your economic possibilities. The challenge itself is very simple, for each week of the year (52 in fact) you will set aside its monetary consideration.

Example: week 1 = 1 €

It is very simple, you start with small amounts to create a habit of saving and then gradually continue until you reach the required amount without having to force yourself too much.

13. 30 days

Simple, before buying something, let 30 days pass. If after 30 days you still want to buy that item then buy it, otherwise no. I can guarantee you that with this method you will not buy 90% of the things that go through your head.

14. Why does it work?

Because in this way you will avoid impulse purchases which are ultimately the ones that steal your wallet. By doing this you will only buy items/experiences you are truly interested in and avoid getting caught up in the consumer syndrome.

15. Extra savings

This third method of saving money consists in becoming "engineers" of one's assets, that is, how to manage money and purchases in full lean and Kaizen style.

16. What's it about?

Easy, make a list of all the regular purchases you have to deal with monthly and understand what you can save on

For example, you can change the telephone rate, electricity supplier, limit the consumption of meat and fish within the shopping cart, declutter your things and sell them to get some extras, the possibilities are endless

17. Why does it work?

Well, it works because we often don't realize how much money we spend, especially when we take out subscriptions. Doing a check now and then can only be good for our wallet.

Caffeine - Detox

OK, if you're caffeine-addicted too, this is more of a challenge than a money-saving method.

What's it about?

Well, the title speaks for itself; stop drinking coffee outside the home. Do people spend at least € 5 a week on coffee at the machine? To which you can add just as many for the coffee at the bar if you usually go there (look for useful data).

Why does it work?

As I said above, the figures speak for themselves! Coffee alone saves € 400 a year. If you can't or don't want to give up the coffee you can do as I do prepare a thermos of coffee and take it to the office. Alternatively, you can try to convince your colleagues to buy a pod machine: it will reduce the cost of coffee and will undoubtedly be of better quality. Another alternative is to cut back on your daily coffee if you drink a lot.

Disclaimer: You can use this strategy for any daily habit you have that makes you spend money. From breakfast at the bar to the purchase of paper newspapers, smoking, etc.

Save cent

This is a saving method that my dad taught me when I was little.

He called it the holiday piggy bank.

How To Save With Minimalism

What's it about?

Whenever you have loose change in your wallet, set it aside. Which and how many depends on you. For example, you could only use the leftovers from the grocery store or the bar, and so on, in the piggy bank. My dad, for example, only uses 1 or 2 euro coins and diligently shoves them into a piggy bank when he has them. The collection for him begins strictly on January 1st and lasts until the day before departure. Based on the content we used to choose the extras of the holiday (such as boat trips, restaurants, etc.)

CHAPTER 13
TEACHING SUSTAINABLE MINIMALISM TO CHILDREN

Why teach children about minimalism?

Think of today's children. Think about society today. This juxtaposition always makes me think a lot because today's children will be the men and women of tomorrow. Today the society we live in is very stressful. Just think of how the job search has become more frenetic, precarious, unstable. Suffice it to say that today, at a fashion level and therefore at a commercial level, there are no longer only 4 seasons but more than 50. What if we look at the backpacks, school supplies, and clothing of our children? We see a great social divide and a lot of competition for the climb to success.

Today we give our kids expensive cell phones and then tablets, consoles, PCs, electronic devices of all kinds. Alt a deep breath. Given that the term minimalism has been coined, or at least spread, quite recently, many people still aren't quite sure what lifestyle it is. Everyone thinks that " minimal " stands for "less" or "renunciation".

In reality, the minimalist philosophy was already known in the past only under a different name. Being minimalist, in the most common sense and not in some extreme form of deprivation, means living WELL with the necessary things to be WELL.

Being a minimalist means detaching oneself from material things, that is, not becoming a slave to them. I'll give a practical example: " oh that skirt is beautiful, I have to buy it!" or " no I can't throw away the notes from middle school, sooner or later I will need them or my children will need them!" Serious? Do you think that in 20 years your children will pick up those notes? Even in elementary school (primary school) everything has now changed. It would make no sense to re-propose outdated notes or methods.

A minimalist means feeling free to move forward without carrying the burden of the hundreds of accumulated things. I tried it on my skin. Being minimal means having priorities and not an agenda that is overflowing with commitments, sometimes even those we don't care about or we know we won't participate in, and they are there to make us anxious every time we turn the pages.

Minimal means letting go, breathing, being grateful for what you have, and buying only what is useful or makes us joyful, which makes us feel good. For me, the transition was also to have fewer material objects but to invest more in experiences. And from here I would engage with the combination of minimalism and children.

Why should you teach children about minimalism?

1) Because replacing material objects with concrete experiences improves relationships within the family and adds quality to life. Even simple but meaningful experiences are enough. Going for a walk instead of staying at home, one in one room and one in another, going out for sports together, parents and children in the

fresh air, taking trips, going to the pool or an exhibition, or attending a children's workshop. Do these things cost?

I am the first one who could not pull at the end of the month but the dress was there, the dinner, the drink, the ballad, the breakfast outside the house were there, creams and scrubs were there, objects just for the sake of having them there, the exit to the shopping center "no, I don't buy anything" and then mysteriously there was bags and small bags. In short, there were many things but then I lacked the money to do something I liked yoga training was too expensive, the vacation was too expensive, attending an event was expensive, taking a cooking class was expensive. But in the end, what added value to my life? The clothes? Creams? Expensive dinners? or maybe I would have given meaning to my life perhaps with that distant destination, that cooking class, the diploma to become a yoga instructor, the show at the theater, or the conference on nutrition? Sure, everyone has their priorities but what information would you prefer to pass on to your children? Who will be successful people with that designer dress or with the right skills given by a training course? Would you like to teach them that hoarding things makes "rich" because they will have so many things or would you like to teach them to invest their money in something that can improve their quality of life? They are choices, hence, establish your priorities.

I assure you that, since I stopped buying junk and useless things, not only have I had the necessary sum to do all the experiences that I had always put off, in addition, I have also advanced. Mind you that 50 euros here, 20 there, 100 and then another 30 slowly make a sum that you would not imagine if you spent them all together.

2) Teaching children about minimalism promotes concentration. Children are continually distracted by the nonsense that does not allow them to concentrate. Upstream is the technological discourse. Children should not study with mobile phones, youtube, TV on, and other sources of distraction. This would already be a step forward. Doing it together is not functional unless they are learning English for example through a cartoon, a funny video, etc. We understood each other!

Furthermore, the study plan should also be free of things that can distract our children and teenagers. A free, clean, and spacious surface leave no room for distractions. Try studying with a desk full of stuff! You will get distracted without complicating anything. (Mettere foto scrivania disordinata) The surface must be clean and shiny after use. We, therefore, teach children and teenagers to put things back where they came from.

3) "One in and one out" rule. How many times are children's rooms full of games, books, trinkets, junk, changes and spare parts, stuffed animals, collectibles? If we removed everything from the cupboards, over the shelves, and from the desk, there would be no more room for us. What are we teaching the children? To have, to have, to have!

We buy a new stuffed animal and we keep all the old ones, we buy a new toy and we never throw one away, we constantly buy clothes but then we keep the old ones "just in case .. ". Here we start from the "case never .." that applies to adults but also children. The "case never" almost always translates to "never".

Teaching Sustainable Minimalism To Children

Since adults choose what to keep and what to sell for clothes, let's make a good selection considering which things your children wear the most and which ones they haven't worn for months if not years. Donate, give away, give away, sell those you don't use. You are not only doing good to others but also yourself. You are freeing up space, don't think about replacing that space right away.

Ditto with the games, ask your children (don't surprise them, it could be a bad surprise for them) which are the 10 games they love the most among the ones they have in the room. Tell them a good story about a journey and a choice of only 10 games. I assure you that after the first moment of difficulty because they would like to keep them all, they will begin to choose those "of the heart". You can also involve them in the donation. Maybe you could physically take the games to places where your gifts are welcome and show them that they are doing a beautiful action! Do a flea market. It will be funny!

Suggest that they find a place for each game or each book so that they know immediately where it is without turning over the house every time they search for something. Teach them to tidy up! However, having space to store them is already a bonus for tidying up. It will all work out in minutes!

4) Having fewer things, consuming less, throwing, or donating with awareness helps both the environment and those who need it. The toy that one child does not use can make another child happy instead of gathering dust. Fewer games and less material to dispose of is a gift for the environment. The people who follow this philosophy of life are also more attentive and respectful of

the environment that surrounds them. For example, children can be taught to use water bottles at school instead of continually using plastic bottles. You can make workshops and games by recycling. You can brush up on the old games of the past where a piece of paper, a pen, and a bit of memory were enough or games of movement games Teach them to have fun with a few things.

5) Thanks to minimalism, children already learn the value of things from an early age. Gifts must be made at the right time. Today, hearing from my students, some parents give out prizes all the time, sometimes even small ones but still prizes and gifts. Reward if you have been good, reward if you got a good grade, reward if you scored a goal, reward if you helped mum or dad to clear the table. While they are small, the rewards may be cheap but as they grow, they certainly won't be.

They must be taught that some things are good to do without necessarily having material feedback instantly and it is equally important to teach them that a relationship is not based on things. Parents do not love their children only when they give gifts and children are not loved. more only when they receive awards. Children especially need you to dedicate time to them. Ask him maybe your children would prefer to do an activity with you, than not have a new toy.

In summary: why teach children about minimalism?

1. To add quality to life: + experiences and - material objects.
2. To ensure order on the surfaces to be used and therefore mental order.

3. To have fewer distractions and thus promote concentration.
4. To learn how to get rid of one thing before taking another home.
5. To establish a precise location for everything.
6. To respect the environment.
7. To transmit the value of sharing, giving, and generosity
8. To find that you can play and have fun even without expensive toys

If we think about it, children are by nature minimalists. They love to play outdoors, draw, dance, ride a bike, play with the ball; instead, they hate cleaning, tidying up, tidying up.

When my daughter was born, I embraced motherhood with the best of intentions. I invested all my energy to give her everything and more. Love, opportunity, safety, fun, entertainment, dialogue, growth, education, healthy food, quality time, and more.

Also, feelings of guilt and inadequacy, because it seems that you can never do enough. In reality, I don't know where mothers' feelings of guilt come from, no one has ever openly told me "you must always play with your daughter and offer her the most incredible things". Then slowly I learned to get rid of so many thoughts, so many useless purchases, and too many commitments.

I happily embraced a simpler approach

I understood that family happiness lies in shared experiences but that everyone, even children, needs moments of solitude, silence, calm, rest, and empty spaces. We spend too much time protecting our children. We would always like to avoid their pain, disappointment, tension, and problems. But unfortunately, our children too must learn that life is also made up of negative things.

We have to manage our fears, let our children live without undermining their trust and autonomy with our fears. We must try to foster their sense of responsibility and enhance their natural curiosity for the world.

Let them play alone without anxiety

We don't have to entertain our children all the time (we don't even have to do the opposite, abandoning them in front of a screen). Working at home, I have often told my daughter that I cannot play with her. After huge feelings of guilt, I noticed how these moments become an opportunity to create and explore new ideas on my own.

When she says to me "I'm bored", I reply that it is excellent news because boredom brings innovation and creativity. She gets a little annoyed, but then she immerses herself in something wonderful.

Let them create

A space full of useless games leaves no room for creativity and free play. An empty, clean and tidy space is a fertile field for invention and imagination.

Let them rest

Every year in September we would like to enroll our children in all extra-curricular courses, in language and artistic workshops. To these are added birthday parties, family commitments, and many other appointments. After a few weeks, we are already tired and stressed. In reality, we just need rest and empty time. Both us and the children.

Rest must become a priority, not a luxury.

We need to learn to plan a lot less and accept fewer invitations (for the good of all). During the weekend at least one of the two days must be completely free of commitments. Reduce the number of sports afternoons (between 3 to 2), compensating for the need to move with an hour of walking a day (30 minutes to go and 30 to return from school).

Let them solve

Children need a lot of practice to learn how to do things and solve problems. We must give them the opportunity and the time to do it, calmly and with serenity. These rules will help us be happier with our children

Remember:

1. Explain to your children that material possessions won't make them happy, as illustrated by the intact toys in their bedroom closet. Talk about living by one's means and not pursuing a life of debt just to maintain a lifestyle. Helping children think about the purchases they make, ask them, "Is this something you need and will use, or do you just want to spend your check?" Let go of the belief that possessing objects is important. Be generous to others so the children can follow your example.

Teaching Sustainable Minimalism To Children

2. Emphasize the benefits of a minimalist life to your children. Say, "Did you notice that it only took a few minutes to clean your room? Now you have more time playing outside!" Encourage your children to live with fewer items, but spend your time focusing on what's important like relaxing together, going to the park, or volunteering as a family. Let them experience the positive benefits of minimalist living without the pressure of giving up everything at once.
3. Avoid filling your schedule with appointments and activities. Predict downtime to get creative, relax, or try something new.
4. Start the battle against the stuff by eliminating what your kids no longer use. Slowly remove other unnecessary items with your child, asking, "Are you planning to use this again?" or, "Do you want to donate this to another child who wants to play with him?" Make piles of items throw, recycle and donate with your child's input. Give sturdy, best-quality gifts to your children in the future that will be lasting. Scan your kids' school and art projects to save them without adding clutter piles to your closets.

5. Set the example of a minimalist lifestyle for your children by getting rid of your excess personal possessions first and shopping for unnecessary items.

Suggestions

Do not force children to dispose of toys and personal items before they are ready. Give them time to see the benefit of a minimalist lifestyle.

6. Keeping a thing as a reminder is fine, but keeping everything as a reminder involves reordering, reorganizing, and wasting time that we can avoid. Space also has a cost whether you have bought your home or are renting it, you should know this well.

7. Do frequent cleaning of what is broken, useless, or that no longer attracts the attention of children (and realize the time spent throwing away things you bought with money earned working).

8. Limit the space where toys can stand. For example, when I notice a toy, a crayon, or a pendant in the same dusty corner of the kitchen or bathroom for more than two days, I throw it away without regret. Nobody ever claims it.

CHAPTER 14
CREATING A MINIMAL WARDROBE FOR CHILDREN

As children grow up, their clothes can pile up and clutter your home. Superfluous things must be eliminated. To keep the room clean, try to organize the remaining clothing by creating a tidy and accessible space for it. Once you've organized their clothes, you'll need to enforce this minimalist lifestyle by taking care of the clothes you currently own without buying any more.

Steps

Method 1: Organize their old clothes

1. Make a list of how many clothes they need: try to identify the types of clothing your child needs and how many of each one needs. Calculate how often you do your laundry to decide how many items of clothing you need.

   You may decide that they need seven casual shirts, three pairs of pants, one dress suit, two hoodies, one coat, one pair of trainers, and two pairs of pajamas.

   Your child's age can also influence this decision. A child may only need three or four different onesie, while a teenager may want a few more outfits.

   Don't forget to consider both winter and summer outfits. You may need seven different shirts for summer than for winter. If you live in a rainy area, you need a raincoat and boots. If your child plays sports, consider the equipment, uniforms, etc.

2. Tidy up all their clothes: go through their entire existing wardrobe to see what you currently own. Make piles of clothes to keep, clothes you want to donate, and clothes you are throwing away. Donate any clothes that no longer fit your child. Places like Goodwill and Salvation Army accept donations of clothes. Local churches, thrift shops, or children's shelters may want them to. If clothing is torn or stained, throw it away. This includes the old underwear. Make the pile of "maybe" clothes

3. Keep plenty of underwear and socks: underwear and socks cannot be reused like other items of clothing. Create a stock of

just over a week for each. A value between ten and fourteen days may be sufficient.

4. Let your child choose which clothes he likes: your child must have a say in what they will keep and what they won't keep. Don't throw out clothing items your child likes to wear or wears repeatedly. Have him choose one or two clothes to keep. If your child has trouble expressing an opinion, ask him how each piece of clothing feels. Do they like how it looks? It is comfortable?

5. Choose items to mix and match: since your child's wardrobe will be much smaller, be sure to choose items that can be combined and matched with as many different outfits as possible. This means keeping at least some neutral garments, such as blue jeans, khakis, and white shirts. Although you may still have colorful or patterned items, this choice will help to match them better.

If your child has a yellow and red striped shirt, he can wear it with khakis or jeans, with a sweater or no sweater, with a long-sleeved shirt under it, or a pullover sweater. If you have a hard time choosing multifunctional clothing, you may choose three or four different colors for your entire wardrobe and miss out on anything that doesn't work with these colors. Older children, especially teenagers, may want to buy more clothes as they start developing their unique style.

Method 2 of 3: Create a tidy space for clothes

1. Choose a space that is easily accessible to children. To help keep things tidy, you should teach your parents how to put their clothes away. While a young child may not understand this right away, you can help by placing their clothes in a place that is easy

for your child to reach and handle. Some ways to keep the space accessible include:
- ✓ Installing a low bar for hanging clothes
- ✓ Place on child-height shelves
- ✓ Using soft-sided bins
- ✓ Hang clothes on child-friendly hangers

2. Install shelves in the closet. Create shelves and drawers in the closet. When the door is closed, clothing is hidden from view. You can do this by adding cubbies or shelves in the closet.

Cubbies with removable containers are easy for children to handle. You can store folded garments inside these. You can even purchase modular cubbies. Modular cubbies are the ones you put together yourself. You just have to buy exactly how many cubes you need or have space for.

3. Hang the warehouse behind the door. The back of the cabinet door can be used for hanging storage. This keeps the room tidy when closed, but provides a great way to individually store things like socks, underwear, scarves, belts, jewelry, and shoes. You can hang a string on the back of the door as a DIY clothesline. Hammer two nails directly across from each other on the back of the door, leaving an inch of space between the nail head and the door. Tie the string to your nails. You can thread scarves and belts over the twine. Command hooks can be attached to the back of a door for jewelry, scarves, belts, or bags. Soft hanging boxes can be used for shoes, underwear, socks, or accessories.

4. Place a laundry basket in their room. To avoid clutter in their bedroom, make sure your child knows where to put their clothes when they are dirty. It can be in a corner, near the bed, or in the

closet. Teach them to always put dirty clothing in the bin when changing. This will prevent the clothes from ruining their room. Teach your kids by showing them where the basket is. If they are young, give them their dirty clothes and say, "Put them in the trash can." Let them do it themselves to learn the habit. Ask him how each piece of clothing feels. If your child has trouble expressing an opinion, ask him how each piece of clothing feels.

Method 3 of 3: Manage with a smaller wardrobe

1. Maintain a strict laundry schedule. Since your child will have fewer items of clothing, you will make more washing machines. Choose one or two days a week to do laundry and apply this schedule so you never run out of clothes.
2. Buy superior quality clothes that last over time. While cheap or used clothing can be affordable and cheap, they may not last very long, forcing you to have to buy even more clothes for your child. Instead, invest in some solid pieces that will last for a while. Sturdy trousers, such as jeans or khakis, are important. If you live in a cool area, buy a good quality winter coat and boots.
3. Reduce the number of clothes you buy. Try to resist buying more clothes for your kids unless they need them. You only buy new clothes when the old ones no longer fit.

    If your child needs new clothes and a holiday or birthday is approaching, you can ask for clothes as a gift. Send your friends and family a list of clothes your kids need along with their sizes.
4. Teach your child to put away their clothes. Even with a small closet, children's clothes can still clutter a room if they are dumped on the floor or tossed around. Teach your child that their

Creating A Minimal Wardrobe For Children

clothes have a "home" to encourage them to store them in the right place. If the clothes are dirty, they go into the laundry basket. If the clothes are clean, they go "home" to the closet or drawers. Teach him: "Dirty clothes go to the bin; clean clothes go to the shelf."

Reinforce this lesson when your child cleans his room by asking questions. You can say, "What's the place for clean clothes?" and wait for them to respond.

5. Teach children to accessorize instead of buying clothes. Older children, especially teenagers, may want to buy more clothes as they start developing their unique style. Instead, encourage them to use accessories to make any outfit unique. As children can go through many stages of fashion, this will prevent unwanted clothing from forming. Some good accessories include:

- ✓ Straps
- ✓ Scarves
- ✓ Hair
- ✓ Jewelry store
- ✓ Gloves
- ✓ Socks

Enforce this minimalist lifestyle by taking care of the clothes you currently own. Once you've organized their clothes, you'll need to enforce this minimalist lifestyle by taking care of the clothes you currently own without buying any more.

Suggestions

Talking to your child about why you are organizing his clothes can help him understand what it means to live minimally.

Some people require more types of clothing than others. Remember that you should judge the wardrobe based on what your child needs. Involve your child, let them decide what to keep, and teach them to take care of their belongings. Make sure any heavy furniture for small children, such as a chest of drawers or freestanding cabinets, is fixed to the wall to prevent it from falling on the child.

CHAPTER 15
CAPSULE WARDROBE: A NEW APPROACH TO WARDROBE

Talking about sustainable fashion means opening Pandora's box. It is based on the selection of a few essential items that follow a chromatic logic and are divided by seasonality. This choice facilitates combinations and allows you to make the most of every single piece, without giving the impression of a boring and monotonous wardrobe.

Does the idea of owning a few clothes upset you? Breathe, let's try to reason. Let's think about how many clothes are in our closet and how many we use. Impulsive purchases, crazy and fanciful items are the ones we use the least

The capsule wardrobe is mostly composed of basic garments, well made and therefore durable over time, in natural materials such as the timeless white cotton shirt to be combined with denim with simple lines or a black knee-length skirt. A wardrobe in which each garment can be combined with at least 5 other combinations without clashing. A container of clothes, elegance, and serenity. Thinking about this, it's not that hard to imagine saying goodbye to frills, sequins, lace, and neon colors.

5 tips

Quality: few but good items. The change of season is an excellent time to identify the pieces we already have that adapt to our needs and on which to rotate future purchases as well.

Natural fabrics: pleasant to the touch and allowing the skin to transpire, such as cotton, linen, jute, hemp if we prefer vegetable fibers, while silk, wool, cashmere, and leather are of animal origin.

Sober colors: easy to combine

Fit and sensations: choosing pieces that enhance the body according to our characteristics and that make us feel good when we wear them is the key to choosing with awareness and joy how to present ourselves to the world. Because yes, sometimes, the dress makes the monk.

No taxation and a lot of common sense: some capsule wardrobe experts have drawn up lists of "mandatory" items, others have set a maximum number of dresses. Virtue, in our opinion, lies in the middle, so we abandon the schemes and try to live our minimalist being with serenity without trapping ourselves in generalizations and restrictions that could become counterproductive. There are useful alternatives to avoid throwing away clothes that we no longer feel are ours, but still in good condition.

Charities: The simplest option is to donate them to a charity, such as Humana, or local Facebook exchange groups.

Physical/online sale: if instead you want to try to sell them, you can turn to second-hand shops - in Italy the Mercatino chain - or to web platforms such as Shedd app or Depop.

Exchange: an excellent opportunity to do business is the alternative of the swap party, we organize ourselves among friends and acquaintances to exchange clothes and accessories, renewing the wardrobe at no cost and without waste.

CHAPTER 16
BE MINIMALIST EVERY DAY

There are 7 main areas in which I apply it (and I'm sure that over time I could increase them, even more, to do better and better!) But for the moment they are:

- ✓ Clothing, shoes, and accessories
- ✓ Food
- ✓ Equipment
- ✓ Furniture, and accessories for the home
- ✓ Apps and programs for the pc
- ✓ Leisure and recreational activities
- ✓ Social media

Clothing, shoes, and accessories

This is perhaps the area in which I can best express my concept of minimalism. About two and a half years ago I decided that I would make a clear change to my way of dressing and to the criteria by which to buy clothing, shoes, and accessories. To tell the truth, I've never been much of a consumer when it comes to clothing. I read some articles that talked about how some of the richest and most influential men in modern history had very simple and minimal wardrobes. Entrepreneurs of the caliber of Steve Jobs, Bill Gates and Mark Zuckerberg, Jack Ma Yun, for example, are among them.

These gentlemen could afford the most expensive clothing on the market, but instead, decide to dress in simple and cheap clothes. Steve Jobs for example, who out of "laziness", if we want to call it that, did not want to occupy his thoughts in the morning in finding the right clothing item for the day and therefore decided that he would buy a sufficient number of the same garment to cover all days of the week and would always wear that.

So he could take the first thing that happened to him, without having to pay attention to the right color combinations or other "rules" imposed by the fashion of the moment.

So I decided to buy a bunch of clothes;

- ✓ 1 pair of shoes
- ✓ 3 pairs of jeans
- ✓ 9 short sleeve shirts
- ✓ 4 long sleeve shirts
- ✓ 3 sweaters

For a total of 19 items. From then on, that was going to be my wardrobe. I did not purchase clothing until the following month of May when I replaced the 9 short-sleeved shirts (black) with as many but in pastel colors, more suitable for fighting the heat of the upcoming summer days.

This allowed me not to spend my time looking for new clothing items to wear, neither online nor around the shops. In addition to saving a lot of money. In the following years, it was enough for me to replace the garments that have worn out over time with as many of the same type \ model.

Food

I like food, I like good food and I like to try new dishes and pairings. I like to share cooking too. What I don't like is wasting food and having the fridge and pantry full of things that I can't consume within a certain time. It has happened to me in the past (who has never?) to buy more food than I could consume before it became unusable (fruit and vegetables for example) and throw them in the trash.

It is a speech that is also worth making for water, but maybe I will make a separate speech about this later on. I try to do is the plan as much as possible what the menu will be for the whole week (with a slight margin of deviation and modification "on the run") so that I can only buy the food that I am sure to consume.

To save money, you don't have to buy junk food but by the right amount. How many times do we buy products on offer which then expire?

Work equipment

It's a moment to find yourself submerged by components that in some cases we will never use. I too had my semi-compulsive buying period in which I was constantly looking for the new. I apply the Pareto principle or the 80 \ 20 law according to which in most cases 80% of an effect is due to 20% of possible causes.

I think this principle is adaptable to any profession that involves owning the equipment. Let's say a blacksmith who owns three welding machines but who then always uses the same one, for example, or who owns five angle grinders but then always finds himself using the same two, let's take a carpenter who owns four circular saws "just in case" but then always use the same cutting table because it is the most functional one. The examples could be many others and on more or less every working area. Apps for mobile phones and tablets and computer programs in the "equipment" category, then the speech could be adapted to practically every profession. "Just in case" are those objects that we keep because they could come in handy in a distant, hypothetical, sometimes non-existent future as TheMinimalists suggest. We don't need these items.

Furniture, furnishings, and accessories for the home

The question is, how do I furnish the house? I feel that I am a little bit favored, perhaps compared to the average, because I don't particularly like furnishing objects, furnishings, and everything that orbits the world of "furniture". I like beautiful, linear, and simple objects and I especially like that they are few, that everyone has their own space and their location within the furniture. This allows me not to accumulate too many and rather try to have as little as possible to maintain linearity and cleanliness in the rooms that belong to me.

Mobile app

Cell phones once didn't have apps. Then came the apps so many apps, more and more apps for everything. They were beautiful, they were colorful, you could finally do with the phone all those things that until then you had been forced to do on the computer, such as managing spreadsheets and pivot tables with Excel, taking freehand notes, writing complex documents with Word, cropping images with photoshop, and many beautiful and very fun other activities, until you realized that doing it on the phone was inconvenient, slow and inaccurate and you went back to doing it as usual on the PC.

Anyway, my dashboard started filling up with apps (like I think anyone over 12's). The apps that I have never, ever, ever used are the ones for making music. I installed them all.

Apps and programs for the pc

Analogous but much more complicated speech for apps and programs for the PC. For these I admit, I still have a lot of work to do and I can improve. I have a lot of software installed, most of which I use for work but I have to admit that I have a lot that I hardly ever use.

If the battery is a tool of virtually infinite size, plugins take this concept, amplify it to the nth power + 1 and shoot it full force like a huge laser beam in the infinite cosmos. Only the sky is the limit (and the space on your hard drives)

Leisure and playful activities

In this section, I enclose all the activities such as cinema, theater, concerts, museums, and other various events. Let's say a little about everything that can be enclosed in the category "cultural activities".

I like to attend in general all the events that I think can convey emotions to me and increase my soul in one way or another. Ok, but how do I know if a business will give me something back if I don't start it first? I don't know.

My being "minimalist" here too lies in the fact that I always choose very carefully which event to attend based on what I believe I will draw from it on an emotional level but without being influenced by fashions or simply by the fact that: "It's Saturday night and therefore we go dancing "or" everyone goes to the So-and-so concert, so I have to go too ",

What I try to do more generally is to let myself be advised more by my instincts than by external inputs, especially if they come from social media.

Social media

Facebook, Twitter, Instagram, Foursquare, Snapchat, Clubhouse, TikTok, etc. although I have an account on each of them, I try to keep away from them as much as possible and not get sucked into the black hole of infinite scrolling. I dedicate a small part of my daily time to "update" on what happens through social networks, but:

I take any news coming from these media as "to be verified"; never come across infinite flames to assert my opinion, I find it a useless waste of time; publish very little, I only do it when I have something to say and I don't expect any likes. This allows me to always remain quite detached from any mood the network wants to pass me at that moment and to close the social network instantly to move on to other things.

Another thing I often do is to rotate the use of social networks, so if I have used Facebook today, tomorrow I will probably not open it but instead, I will use Instagram, Twitter, or maybe neither. There are whole days in which I happen not to open any social network. The only media I really can't live without is YouTube, which though:

- it cannot be defined as a social network
- I use it basically to learn new things

However, digital minimalism is a much more complex topic than that and I think I'll write more about it in a future article. Have you ever eaten on a table cluttered with other things? Not to resist during the sales and to buy things that you don't need? Has it ever happened to you to buy that shirt or leggings that the influencer had sponsored, but then it didn't look so good on you and you got frustrated? How did it go? Have you found yourself in any of these questions? Minimalism for me means, adding rather than removing, that is, having fewer things around, fewer clothes in the wardrobe, less mess in the head, to have more energy, more creativity, and more clarity. LESS IS MORE or LESS is MORE

Principle Of Improvement By Subtraction Applied To Life

The expression used by a great master of architecture Ludwig Mies Van Der Rohe in the context of a minimalist style to be reached through A WORK OF SUBTRACTION in a CREATIVE PROCESS of continuous SEARCH FOR SIMPLICITY to ADD QUALITY " Less is more "is that more than comes from less.

Now we transpose it from architecture to mind and body and also to lifestyle. Yes, I like to think of minimalism with a holistic approach. Let's see in practice how to apply it and you will also find my approach

Wardrobe: fewer clothes, more decisions, more creativity in creating outfits If you buy consciously, that is, you buy what you need and take interchangeable and combinable garments, you will actually have fewer clothes in the closet, but more creativity and also less energy expenditure. For example, I buy things that make me feel at ease, without letting myself be influenced by the dictates of fashion.

By doing this, I also reduce stress, yes, I don't waste time choosing what to wear or trying on clothes that I have in the closet, but that half of the dress which I no longer used, but I keep them there in the hope of putting them back on. Body changes and also our tastes, I prefer to immediately select everything and what I did not wear the previous year or give it to a friend or give it or sell it at every wardrobe change.

You minimize the decision fatigue, and this mode is useful not only for clothing but applies to all other sectors, such as the refrigerator for example or the pantry or the office

Desk: If you work from home or in the office, the less you see on the table, the greater your concentration (put photos of the messy desk) When I started to approach this system, I started looking at images of desks on Pinterest and I came across those cool photos of desks with only a pc, a notebook and a pen, at most a map, there I was dazzled, it was what I needed. I discovered then that the lean desk, free and clean, would become my mood and so it is, today I don't dream of starting to work or write in the casino, the chaos outside reflects the chaos inside

But sometimes, in moments of creativity, when I have to design courses or lessons, then I scatter everything around, but it's only because that way I find the ideas, but immediately after everything returns to its place and my rule is this: " one-touch "that is, I touch and put it back.

As I do?

I no longer buy a thousand notebooks and then not use them, today I choose my notebooks with care, because they are both my fundamental work tools, but also "clear heads", and I buy them when I no longer have anything to write on. It applies to pens, I buy them all the time, but I buy the ones I know I will use, and even in this case I choose them consciously In this way, there is an incredible saving and you buy things of higher quality!

Minimalism and Mind

Now let's talk about two processes that cause stress and how a more minimalist approach can help improve the situation and reduce anxiety.

1. **Over-thinking:** having redundant thoughts, brooding, being indecisive, causes psycho-physical stress and energy consumption and often leads nowhere, undecided between thinking and doing. When you feel your mind so cluttered and the thoughts that run speak to yourself saying "Stop".

   Take a deep, diaphragmatic breath, that is, place a hand on your abdomen, listen to the breath grow in your belly, then return to your body. Stay with your mind in the here and now and take back control.

   As I do?

   I write a list of all the things I have in mind (the famous "empty head" notebook I mentioned earlier) "If you can't do it right away, WRITE IT" Then I evaluate the thoughts that I have written, projects, fears, things that I am putting off and I put myself in action mode, instead of thinking I do. So you clear your mind and also become incredibly more productive. Constantly thinking about something we want to do, and then we don't do, makes us waste days and hours. Fewer thoughts, more action

2. **Multitasking:** doing many things together you waste energy and time. Yes, so at SINGLE TASKING fewer things, but done well!

Minimalism and Body

Having a MINDFUL approach, that is aware, being present in what you do, inhabiting the body. LITTLE AND OFTEN Even strictly physical work for me uses the same principle, little by little is better than time and time again, I prefer to create my training plans starting from the easy, little by little, 15 minutes of physical activity daily, rather than 2 hours twice a week.

These are also the principles of Laizen, the Japanese mechanism of progressive improvement, I accustom the body to train and move gradually and pleasantly.

What do I do?

While I walk, I just walk, while I train, I train and I stay in my body, if the thoughts arrive, and they do arrive, then I move them for a moment in a corner of the mind. With practice it becomes inevitable, you never go back because the benefit is tangible

Purchases To Improve, Compensate, Cover Minimalism, and Acceptance

We buy new clothes especially when we don't feel good about ourselves;

1. **Unintentional Purchases**
   The non-acceptance of the body leads to seeking elements of compensation and, remaining on the subject of material things, it will be clothes, accessories, shoes, an accumulation of things that compensate you at that moment, but then, the situation returns.

Then there is the strong media stimulus, which invites you to buy clothes and make-up, dissociating yourself more and more from your body and inviting you, indirectly, to want to resemble those aesthetic models proposed. This generates frustration, insecurity and feeds the continual search for other things to try to compare you

Thus, it happens that the attention is completely outside of you, it is shifted to material resources, to build a reality on the surface and each offer is not limited only to the object itself, but to the construction of your being, of an identity. They take advantage of your desire to change.

What do I do?

I stop to recognize my primary resources and when I want to buy I ask myself two questions

- "Do I need this purchase? "
- "What value does it add to me?"

You have to learn to choose what you want.

2. **Unintentional Physical Activity**

Over-training! Overtraining to get to a result, to get perfection, to get to a very specific aesthetic canon, to no longer love the body. You should train intentionally, to progressively improve, to feel flexible, strong, and healthy. Minimalism here is understood as love for the body, respect, and care, dosing fatigue, effort, returning to inhabit the body, and recognizing that the body does wonderful things that we realize when we miss them. Do not look for a thousand Christian-smashing workouts, accumulating saved videos, other people's files, work on yourself by dosing your energies with a view to progressive improvement for a healthy body and not to have everything immediately, the body is like nature, it has his times. We have to listen to our bodies.

All these actions of subtraction will lead to a greater benefit in your body;

- To energy and economic saving.
- Less stress.
- Less anxiety and more energy.
- Start by becoming aware of this less phrase is more - less is more and start evaluating the waste in your life
- Start with a specific area.
- Start by buying a notebook, or see if you already have one at home, and write down everything you would like to change/modify/replace.
- I have a "wish list" where I mark the things I like / need/want and as I assign them to me, that is often when I set myself a goal, I give myself a gift.
- As for your body, write down the things you want to change and work on, overthinking we have seen how expensive it is and leads nowhere, don't tell you all the time I should lose weight or exercise, write it down now and plan it.

CHAPTER 17
MINIMALISM SKINCARE

The minimalist approach finally comes to skincare. The Skin is born Minimalism, or Skinimalism, to take care of your skin in a few targeted steps. How many times have we found ourselves making room in our wardrobes, getting rid of clothes that we don't wear, or that "don't give us joy" as Marie Kondo teaches?

What happens when this attitude applies to skincare?

Lately, in the beauty community, we are starting to talk about skins minimalism, or minimalism, a term that describes an essential approach to the skincare routine. What exactly does it consist of?

Skin minimalism, as the word itself suggests, is based on minimalism; the skin has few needs that can be largely satisfied with the use of a few effective products, included in a fast and minimal routine.

What makes this approach successful is undoubtedly the ease with which it adapts to the demanding lifestyle of many of us, finally offering us an alternative to the complicated and time-consuming routines that involve the use of many products, often similar to each other. they. But skin minimalism or minimalism is much more than this; it means a more edited and intelligent routine, made up of a few essential products and above all aimed at achieving a result.

But the skin does minimalism work? Can a minimalist routine work on the skin?

Here is our answer: absolutely yes, as long as you choose the right products. Minimalist skincare does not simply mean using a few products randomly chosen from the shelves of a perfumery. It means taking the time to listen to your skin, understand what it needs, and then turn to targeted products, capable of enhancing its natural beauty.

Choosing beauty minimalism above all means giving up layering and complex passages. An advantage also for the skin: the wrong combination of ingredients could trigger irritation and allergic reactions, making the beauty routine very ineffective. The wrong combination of exfoliating acids, for example, could make the skin hypersensitive, and excessive layering weighs it down, making skincare much less pleasant. The less approach is more to skincare, then, is perfect for giving the skin everything it needs, observing which ingredients are beneficial. Give up some cosmetics or choose 2-in-1 formulations.

The Real Needs Of The Skin

Cleansing, exfoliation, hydration, and protection. The skin doesn't need anything else to be healthy. And, precisely for this reason, minimalist skincare can only be based on four fundamental steps. A very important step is cleansing, to be performed morning and evening, to eliminate excess sebum, pollution, and dirt from the skin, allowing subsequent treatments to penetrate more deeply.

Equally essential, hydration allows the skin to remain young and vital, luminous. In both cases, customization cannot be missing: every skin type needs specific ingredients and textures.

The skin also needs to be renewed through exfoliation. Eliminating dead cells through a scrub, a peeling, or, simply, an exfoliating tonic has, in fact, an illuminating effect and allows better oxygenation of the tissues. The last step of minimalist skincare can only be protection; the SPF is the best anti-aging in existence and allows you to keep the skin healthy.

The Must-Have Products In Skincare

The minimalist approach to skincare manifests itself in the form of different beauty trends, above all Skinimalism. A vision of skincare that is based on reducing the number of cosmetics in the beauty routine. In the center? The multitasking formulations.

A very different approach from that of Skincare, which re-evaluates what the skin needs by literally skipping a few steps. A trend that comes from Korea and that immediately involved millennials, eager to reduce waste generated by the cosmetics industry. Minimalist skincare by definition, whose cornerstones are cleansing and hydration. At the heart of Skincare, there is the health of the hydrolipidic film, capable of regulating skin hydration and defending the skin from free radicals. The key, in both cases, is the ingredients. The skin can never lack Vitamin A, E, and C, as well as a series of antioxidant substances.

CHAPTER 18
MAKE-UP DECLUTTERING

What is decluttering make-up for? How to choose what to keep and what to throw?

Decluttering make-up is nothing more than the reordering of our make-up and the workstation dedicated to them. The usefulness of decluttering make-up is easy to say: we get rid of products that we no longer use or have expired, and make room for new tricks!

In general, having a well-organized make-up station is essential because it allows us to achieve many different looks, using products that we thought we no longer had or that remained hidden "under the heap". There are some criteria of choice, such as reading the cosmetic PAO or observing them understand if they are still usable or could give us adverse reactions to the skin.

There comes a time when decluttering make-up becomes a necessity. If the make-up is overflowing and we realize that we don't use everything we have, well, it's time to tidy up! The philosophy of decluttering tricks is very useful, girls because by getting rid of unused objects we will also make order in our mind, freeing up space for our creativity and why not some new product that we are sure we will use. To reorganize the make-up and make-up station we have to ask ourselves some very useful questions, such as "is it expired?", Or "do I use it?".

Why do decluttering make-up? What is it for reorganizing the tricks?

Girls, as we said, reorganizing make-up with decluttering is a necessary operation, to be done 2/3 times a year. First of all, it helps us to identify, and therefore throw away, all the expired make-up that could be non-performing or even harmful to our skin.

To understand if a product is to be thrown away, our advice is to attach special labels on the bottles bearing the opening date: in this way, then reading the PAO on the back, to immediately understand if that given product is "safe" or must Leave. The PAO reports the life of the product from its opening: indicating that,

Otherwise, another way to understand whether to keep or let go of a product is to observe it, smell it, and spread it; regardless of the PAO, if a cosmetic has been stored poorly it may have expired prematurely.

The usefulness of make-up decluttering is therefore linked to the exclusive use of "good" products, which have not gone bad and with good performance.

Furthermore, organizing the tricks with decluttering allows us to understand if we have actually "exaggerated" with the make-up shopping, buying too many cosmetics that we will not even have time to use before their expiration.

How To Set The Decluttering Make-Up: What To Have Available To Start The Make-Up Make-Up

To begin with, we advise you to use a room or an area of the house for tidying up cosmetics: better to avoid staying in the bathroom, which normally has smaller spaces and could make us a little too messy!

The ideal is to get an old blanket to place on the ground, on which to subsequently spread all the "content" of our make-up station, dividing the products according to the category they belong to (for example eye shadows, mascara, blush, lipsticks and so on).

Better to have on hand also:

- A garbage bag, for expired and irrecoverable cosmetics
- Some transparent plastic boxes, for the tricks we decide to give away
- Beauty case for the ones we choose to keep.

In addition to products that have expired or gone bad, how do you decide who goes and who stays?

In the meantime, let's make a list of the indispensable products. An example? For the make-up base we might need:

- ✓ One - two foundations (based on texture, for example, a liquid and a compact powder)
- ✓ A concealer for dark circles and one for pimples
- ✓ A couple of blushes
- ✓ Earth or bronzer
- ✓ Face powder
- ✓ Illuminating

For the eyes always useful:

- ✓ A mascara
- ✓ An eyeliner
- ✓ Some colored and black kajal pencil
- ✓ Two-three eye shadow palettes in shades that we use: nude or more vibrant colors

Don't forget the lips: here the list would be useless because everyone likes playing with colors! So to do the decluttering lipsticks we think about what suits us best (if you want to learn more we have a blog post that talks about how to choose the red lipstick based on the color scheme) and the finishes that we need most. For example, if we spend a lot of time at home we might adore creamy ones, if we often wear the mask we will tend to prefer lip colors or very long-lasting and opaque colors.

In Addition To The Essentials, We Also Keep Extraordinary Products For More Particular Looks

Once you have identified the must-have products from our makeup collection, it's time to decide what to throw away and what to give; in the latter case, be careful because not all cosmetics are suitable for donation. For example, absolutely no mascara or eyeliner. The rest can be disinfected with pure alcohol.

Conclude The Decluttering: In Order Not To Create Disorder, We Use Organizer And We Have Everything With Criteria

At the end of the make-up decluttering moment to buy less and better our cosmetics, girls! The world of makeup is wonderful, but waste is always a shame, from many points of view. So let's try to buy only what we are safe to use. Returning to the topic, how to make the decluttering of our cheat collection effective? The answer is to try to organize them better so that we have at hand what we use on a daily or at least weekly basis.

Make-up Decluttering

The make-up organizers are very useful, to be placed on our make-up station or in the bathroom on the various shelves. An idea could also be to prepare a box containing our TOP of the period (for example foundation, concealer, and mascara) to have everything at hand in the same place.

CHAPTER 19
APPLY MINIMALISM TO THE KITCHEN

※≈◎◎≈※

Many know about minimalism applied to art and furniture, but there is also a culinary one that also helps not to waste. Food is not entertainment. Food is fuel, pure and simple. This doesn't mean I don't like the food I enjoy it immensely.

There is a frequent image that describes minimalism, it is an empty room with white walls and a chair. "I have a bed, a chair, and a radio. I'm the one who decides if something adds value to my life", he says Joshua Fields Millburn from inside his large American house, now half-empty. With Ryan Nicodemus, he created The Minimalists, released two documentaries on Netflix, a long series of podcasts, a blog, and several books. In their bio, the two claim to have helped "more than 20 million people live a more meaningful life" with fewer things.

Minimalism is not born with them but instead develops in art, more specifically in the 60s, in America which reacts to Pop-Art and proposes a new style in which simple and essential lines, elementary designs, and geometric modules predominate. Hence the minimalist approach could broaden the gaze to also invest in music and literature and bounce back to our 20s in the form of existential minimalism. No longer just art but a lifestyle that adapts and reacts to the drifts of the 2000s consumerism, in particular, the compulsive possession of goods, the obsession with money and career, waste.

The aim is not to waste

Cooking is one of my greatest loves. Not always, I wasn't one of those genius little girls who could cook a Wellington fillet at eight. Well, let's say that before getting engaged I never touched a pan, but from then on light came on and something inside me glimpsed the immense and spectacular world of cooking. Without boring you with my culinary journey, taking the path of minimalism meant putting my concept of cooking and my style in the kitchen back in place.

Cooking is in itself a minimalist art

Avoid buying ready-made, processed, and processed products, avoid drowning among the packages and parcels in the pantry, work the raw material from its essence (flour, butter, sugar, eggs), it has a very strong minimalist component. The home cooking, that of the grandmother, frugal, made of recovery, of "nothing is thrown away" is a real philosophy of life and those who embrace it are already embracing minimalism.

1. Avoid processed food, go back to basics and cook real food with your own hands right from the basic preparations. Learning to cook basic preparations, for example, has produced in me an extra awareness of how often you buy completely useless stuff, which does not help either in time or even less in health. I have often found that a basic dough takes a few minutes and simple steps, so in the end I find myself not having to buy ready-made food anymore, I don't have to stock up just because I might need it and I enjoy real, healthy food, made with ingredients I know and that I can also keep in right quantities for future occurrences when I don't have time

2. You have to buy what is necessary. Transforming and storing your food is a healthy habit that serves not to waste abundance, not to waste scraps, and to have supplies of real food in exchange for prepackaged equivalents. However, this must keep us far, indeed very far from accumulation. The handouts for "shopping crazies" are the anti-minimalism par excellence, the result of the compulsive accumulation of large-scale retail objects that often do not even serve us.

3. Minimalism in the kitchen is to transform and work your food to preserve it without wasting it. As above, transforming extra food, scraps, or leftovers and carefully storing a little stock is practically an art (for example, I'm not as good as my grandmother at making jars, but that's it). Knowing exactly what

has been set aside, knowing that nothing has been wasted of what has been hard-earned, knowing that if necessary we will have something to draw on, is relaxing for the mind, it is order and security in one's means.

4. Minimalism in the kitchen is aiming for zero waste or, more generally, not wasting.
5. Minimalism in the kitchen means abandoning large-scale distribution as much as possible and returning to consciously choosing one's food.

    I still set foot at the discount store, sometimes, to buy raw materials that I have no way to get, otherwise, I buy everything elsewhere, in theory, it should be bought; meat from the butcher, fish from fisherman, fruit, and vegetables from the farmer. It is not a snobbish choice, on the contrary, I know what to buy and how it is produced.
6. Follow the cycle of nature, eat in season and preferably local food. The mental order of minimalism also benefits from following the cycle of nature. Indeed, often the detachment of our ego that causes anxiety and frustration and drags us into the abyss is caused precisely by the fact that according to modern society it always seems that we live at the same time.

    Air conditioning all year round, all food always available all year round, work cycles with the same peaks all year round, prevent us from "Being", from perceiving our presence here and now and calming our mind. The confusion of not feeling present brings anxiety, stress, the desire to fill our gaps with purchases, that perennial feeling of dissatisfaction that minimalism has always tried to extinguish.

Feeling the season through food serves to feel more present and more serene. Then I also consume food that comes from abroad but I don't make it my main source of livelihood; let's say that I don't live on avocado (as fashion dictates) and I don't eat red peppers in December (except the ones that I have saved on purpose to enrich the winter cuisine from time to time). So here too nothing snobbish, we just try to be more aware of where we live and what season it is, moreover, always speaking in terms of minimal, I already go out knowing which fruit or vegetables I want to buy or having a limited choice, and it is infinitely relaxing for the mind not having to choose one among ten thousand vegetables but only one among those offered by the season.

7. Take care with food so as not to get messed up afterward between medicines, doctors, and pharmacies. A true, healthy cuisine, rich in variety, which follows the seasons and which thrives on the commitment of cooking food for oneself and the pantry with one's own hands, leads to an incredible return to health. Whenever I have a problem with those banalotti, let's say for which one would use over-the-counter drugs and at most the google consultation, I study the way to better balance my kitchen and my minimal home pharmacy always thanks.

8. Surround yourself with what you need, only use tools and accessories in which to invest your money well.

Apply Minimalism To The Kitchen

I am a huge fan of technological tools, I admit. However, I strongly believe in surrounding ourselves only with useful things that truly improve our lives. When I went to live together officially, in my first home, I found myself with packs and packs of kitchen items of very little use until the time came for the decluttering of drawers and cabinets, and there I found you; mashers, cut them, cook eggs, one hundred pans one hundred other pans so huge they don't even get the heat on the fire, pans that were not suitable for induction (which I had), milk pans (which I do not drink), two herbal teas, three coffee machines (including this 1 and 12), a yoghurt machine, an electric crepe maker and twenty ceramic cheese knives.

Now, you will understand the discomfort of discovering that, for example, I didn't even have a can opener. That said, the decision was unanimous: away (usually at the flea market) everything that has no real use or that can be replaced sensibly. So things like the yoghurt machine replaced with a multi-purpose container and a warm place in the house, the bread machine replaced with my hands and the traditional oven, the garlic press replaced with nothing ... nobody needs one. On the other hand, having made a lot of space, and left only one pan for each type and size that is used at home, here is the place to put a lot of really useful things that we didn't buy because we already had the crammed cabinets: planetary mixer, multifunction robot, programmable pressure cooker, slow cooker, vacuum machine, meat, and sausage grinder, etc. I have a lot of kitchen items, really, but all are used constantly, kept well, and the fantastic dishes that allow me to cook pay off every single euro spent.

Study, search, learn, experiment without losing your mind

Open your mind, never stop studying new foods, cultures, processing and conservation methods, techniques. Try recipes, create your style, and most of all, make room in your head and in your home for all the amazing things to come.

CHAPTER 20
THE THOUGHT OF FUMIO SASAKI

Who is Fumio Sasaki ?

Fumio Sasaki is the author of the book "Make Room in Your Life." Fumio Sasaki is Japanese, as the name suggests. Fumio is a young man under 40 who works in the publishing world. Today we are talking about him and above all about his choice to live in the most absolute minimalism. Her lifestyle was documented and described in the book *Make Room for Your Life*. In this book, he explains his motivation and the advantages that came from this extreme choice in a hyper-consumerist world.

In his small studio of just 35 square meters, we find very few objects. In all, she can satisfy her needs with just 20 items, as you'll find out in the book. All objects that Fumio needs, are counter-current choice, minimalist choice, and courageous choice.

For Asian culture, living in simplicity is good and right. For example, for the Japanese, freeing themselves from uselessness leads to rediscovering the meaning of things.

If we then add the Zen Buddhist influence and their teachings we can reap incredible benefits in this regard. In this case, we invite you to delve into Zen Buddhism and the benefits it will bring to your wallet.

We want to give a little introduction. The first teaching of Zen Buddhism leads us to simplify and remove useless objects. Removing objects means reducing our emotional attachment to those objects. And emotional attachment leads us to suffer in the event of a lack of that good. Reducing attachment leads to liberation and takes us away from suffering. Owning fewer items will lead to a reduction in suffering. Just wellness? No, a minimal life improves the lives of those who want it. A minimal life brings big advantages:

- Organization: You will have a better-organized home.
- Well-being: by living in an orderly house you will acquire a feeling of well-being.
- Savings: the minimal style imposes a strict choice on purchases, so you will save a lot.

Because this book is for you

In this case, we are talking about ten euros well invested. The expense is definitely worth the game. In this world made only of objects, where we find pleasure only in material things, a book like this is a panacea for our well-being and to drastically improve the quality of our life.

We associate pleasure with the value of the object possessed. We want more and more and our lives pile up with useless objects and loaded with sentimental value. Learning to eliminate, to cancel, and above all not to buy, can make a huge difference. If you are still undecided, take it now and learn to rediscover the value of small things and their benefits.

I too was a compulsive hoarder. In my native home, I found the whiskers of my first cat preserved. I kept everything for fear of forgetting. I kept everything in order not to detach myself from the affections. To not have

The Thought Of Fumio Sasaki

to say goodbye. Thanks to Fumio Sasaki I learned that "in a house where there are few things, there can be happy".

Most of the items we have are not important to us. And to be able to take possession of those unnecessary items we employ a great deal of work and money. This same reasoning is present in Andrea Bizzocchi's book "Vivere senza lavoro".

When you have too many things, you can't keep up with each of them; then with all that clutter it becomes difficult to clean and the space in which you live is always a little dirty and unkempt: this helps to undermine self-confidence and the desire to do.

The book lists 55 rules for getting rid of things, plus another 15 for eliminating even more things. "What is important, however, remains with us". Some say that if you eliminate things you also give up your past, but I don't believe in such an exaggeration. The key memories of our life naturally remain etched in us.

I'd rather spend my money on an experience than on objects. Experiences raise the quality of life and cannot be compared with other people's experiences because they are unique. Read it if you want to lighten your life.

CHAPTER 21
CONCLUSIONS

It is enough to open a newspaper or watch a news program to see that the world is collapsing, waste is submerging us and the relocation of companies creates numerous abuses and victims. When I heard the word "minimalism" I was reminded of marble, white color, an empty house, and a deep green indoor plant. A stock image of some service that sells photos on the internet.

We are led to associate several concepts with this word:

The minimalism of rich white men (Americans): six-zero bank balance, house finished in marble, Macbook, iPhone, and refined furniture.

Nomadic and wildlife: unlike the first case, here we are reminded of the 50-liter backpack that contains everything you own, vans, trips to the Pacific. If you are not a rich American or a nomad you are screwed. But this is not the case. There are no established rules and anyone can start this path rich, poor, white, black, static, and dynamic. It can be applied to everyday life, to adventurous life, to any type of existence. So forget everything and start over with the fundamental questions.

What is minimalism?

A current, a lifestyle. Those who follow him at first eliminate everything they own and believe is in excess and a second moment avoids falling back into the error of possessing things in excess.

Is the aim to have as few items as possible?

The aim is to have only really useful items or what you want to have.

Are we only talking about material things?

No! Objects represent one of the first steps. What we decide to buy, however, speaks volumes about the people we are, and starting with eliminating what we possess of material triggers a large number of more intimate and abstract reflections that will affect the rest of life as well.

What are the areas in which minimalism can be applied?

Whole life and Anything.

Does being minimalist means having to think a lot?

Yes, think and reflect. Not only that, but it also implies learning to know each other thoroughly and changing one's vision. Why should I follow him?

The fewer the worries, the better life gets. The fewer things you have to do, the more time you can use for what you love. The benefits it brings are undeniable and experienced by all those who voluntarily decide to start this path (the same cannot be said for those who are forced and consequently do not have the right mental predisposition). It is a way to grow, to question oneself, and to get to know each other deeply. To make room to fill with what truly makes life worth living.

How to become a minimalist?

As I said earlier, there is no magic formula or handbook to be meticulously followed. There can only be advised to get started and to continue. Mind you, however, they are just tips that are suggestions that you can customize, increase or modify to your liking.

- Start by writing a list of the things you feel are yours.
- Do a first declutter of the house and everything you own.
- Starting with objects is certainly the wisest choice.

Make a first complete declutter of your home. Dividing it by categories and not by rooms is more convenient because it allows you not to eliminate the same things placed in different environments but to do everything at once, so you don't have to think about it again.

You can proceed like this, starting from things you love least to go gradually towards objects that are usually more symbolic and full of meaning:

- Utensils and kitchen materials (sets of dishes, tablecloths, and so on)
- Small appliances and technology + accessories (e.g. phone covers, cables you don't know what they connect to)
- Household linen (sheets, towels, blankets, etc)
- Personal hygiene products, toiletries, and makeup
- Medicines
- Stationery and the like
- Paperwork (bills, payments, notices)
- Various things (drawers where everything ends, closets)

Conclusions

- Ornaments and souvenirs
- Clothes, shoes, and accessories
- Collectables (DVDs, CDs, video games, and the like) and books
- Do not rush
- Use what you have until its end comes

Consume what you love to the fullest. Do not surround yourself with useless things, and if you have them, give them up by throwing them away or giving them away / selling them (if they are in good condition).

Use the things you love. If you can fix what is not working properly

My PC, about a year ago, looked dead. It did not turn on and when, miraculously, it did, the keys did not work properly. I could have replaced it but I decided to fix it. It has been fixed and the keyboard has been changed. After a year I am writing again thanks to him. Until they tell me there is nothing more to do, I will continue to keep it.

- Create a welcoming environment
- Make your home as comfortable as possible
- Throw away the superfluous and take advantage of the spaces. Keep it tidy
- Clean up inside your car

Think about whether you can also do without a car using public services. Think about how many problems and hassles you would save yourself. If you can't give up the machine, it eliminates all the dirt that accumulates inside it. Finished water bottles (maybe use a water bottle), handkerchiefs, bubble gum packets, and more. Even the car is an environment that must convey serenity.

Cut out unnecessary and harmful activities

Social

When I think of malicious activities, social media immediately comes to mind. I am referring in particular to unnecessary comments, discussions, and articles. Time spent reading free spite and hate. This is the first activity that I would advise you to cut and reduce.

The rubbish tv

The same rule applies to social networks. TV has reached an awkward level when it comes to content. Enjoyable programs can be counted on the fingers of one hand. The same goes for streaming platforms, not everything is to be thrown away but it would at least be reduced. Consuming content one after another, betting on episodes, does not enrich us in any way. Don't look so much to do.

Unwanted communications

Newsletters, hammer advertising, App notifications, Whatsapp groups where 150 useless messages are equivalent to useful information. Trash everything, unsubscribe and leave.

The vices

Smoke, scratch cards, machines, compulsive eating. These activities take a lot of time and money away from us, never leading to anything good. When they become a real problem we have to turn to a specialist and, with a little effort, we will see our lives improve.

Events you don't want to attend

Don't you feel like having an aperitif with Tizio because you planned to read that beautiful book waiting for you on the table? Decline the offer without guilt. We don't always want to do what others propose. Better not to go than to do it reluctantly,

Use the time for what you enjoy doing

- Avoid doing things that don't bring any value
- Try to think about what could happen if you spent most of your free time chasing that dream you have in your drawer, or studying to improve in a discipline you like. Not with eagerness and anxiety, but with pleasure and profit.
- Think of your efforts all went in a certain direction how many improvements and milestones you could achieve. You can do it, just eliminate all those activities that lead nowhere. Calmly, however, do not get caught up in the frenzy otherwise you get exhausted. It also takes moments of pure relaxation.

Manage personal relationships

Sore spot Personal relationships are very complicated. The primary advice is to spend your time with positive people who help us grow, inspire us and treat us well. Toxic relationships, as we all know, lead nowhere.

Being a minimalist means cultivating the right level of self-love. You don't eliminate anyone from your life just because they have flaws. Only people who prove harmful on many fronts are eliminated. It means choosing people to cultivate the positive ones that we like and enrich us and make us spend quality time and eliminate the harmful ones that suck our time and energy, without giving anything in return,

Relationship management is something very personal, everyone experiences them differently because they think differently, have different types of emotionality, and have various levels of tolerance. Don't hang out with people just to do, to fill in the time gaps. It would not be respectful for each other and not even for you. Learn to be alone. Your own company is better than randomly chosen companies.

Choose carefully who to dedicate yourself to

We must try to work on the less pleasant aspects of our minds and character. Smooth the sharp corners, eliminate the automatisms that make us always react in the same way.

Changing what surrounds us and our activities is already a way to free the mind from a great deal of uselessness. Throwing away items and reducing the stress brought on by social media, TV, and whatnot is a small step forward. We cannot limit ourselves to the material side of minimalism. I can combat anxious and obsessive thoughts by writing. Pursuing a goal and trying to realize your projects improve life at 360°, instills security, and makes us feel the best version of ourselves.

When you relax, you relax

For many, the "relaxing moment" is on the sofa, shaking the home of social media. Do you think it's relaxing? No, it's a constant bombardment of the brain. Information left and right. To relax, try to detach yourself from everything, do a single activity that is truly rejuvenating for your poor neuronal connections. Detach from the bombing, turn off everything, forget about the existence of the phone, notifications, and continuous updates.

Improve sleep

In quantity and quality, sleeping well is essential to function properly throughout the day. There are some tricks you can use like:

- ✓ Avoid screens before bed
- ✓ Don't set your alarm as the last thing of the day
- ✓ Making the bedroom environment as relaxing as possible
- ✓ Use breathing and relaxation techniques
- ✓ Be regular in the hours

Improve nutrition

We can reduce what we eat, eat only quality food, eliminate most of the meat and prefer seasonal fruit and vegetables. It is also better to cook simple dishes, slightly spicy, light to digest. Drink lots of water, avoid what is industrial, high-calorie, rich in dyes and preservatives. Bring a large amount of fiber, reduce lactose and carbohydrates.

Exercise (or something similar)

Even just 10 minutes a day. A walk with the dog, some exercise, whatever. Physical activity stimulates the production of hormones, in particular, endorphins and hirsin; the former is considered the hormone of happiness, the latter useful for preventing dementia, burning fat, and strengthening bones.

What happens once we have done all of this?

Here comes the best. This long list of things to improve and eliminate is just the means to an end. Many believe that this is minimalism: throwing away, reducing, erasing, making room. But minimalism, the real one, is what comes next.

Having things that we like, being with people who satisfy us, no longer having the feeling of wasting time, but feeling that we like the things we do, enrich and satisfy us, make us better. In short, minimalism is about giving a better quality to one's life.

Minimalism, for me, is a life worth living, tailor-made for us, without external conditioning. It is spending the time we have truly understood who we are, and not as strangers to ourselves. It is letting go of what others want.

The key idea of minimalism is to get rid of those that don't add value to our life, to make room for what does. For example, eliminate clutter, distractions, and unhealthy relationships, and leave more room for things that are essential to our well-being, such as creativity, love, and play.

Minimalism or minimalist living leads you to intentionally focus on what's important and put the rest aside. In other words, it's about enjoying life more, having less.

Put aside everything that doesn't make you feel good: get rid of everything that gets in your way, everything that distracts you, that makes you lose focus. Get rid of everything that takes away your calm and clarity. Instead, stick to what contributes to your well-being.

- Don't buy things you don't need: don't be fooled by advertising, fashions, and the opinion of others. Having more things will not make you happier. The truth is that when we have enough to meet our basic needs, material possessions cannot improve our well-being in any way. They can only grant us a momentary gratification that disappears very soon, leading us into a worse psychological state.
- Appreciate what you have: Focus on what you have rather than what you lack. Otherwise, you will always feel incomplete, dissatisfied, and a prisoner of your desire.
- Minimize digital distractions: e-mail, instant messaging, social networks, recreational browsing... All this distracts you and makes you lose focus, attention on the present moment. Use digital means consciously and monitor interactions with other people.
- Improving interpersonal relationships: in the age of the internet, which facilitates interconnection, we are increasingly disconnected. We lack real human relationships, real ones.
- Doing one thing at a time: a minimalist life means living focused. In other words, enjoy every moment to the fullest. If we are always distracted and/or linked to multitasking, it will not be possible.
- Focus on Important Goals: Most people generally have a large number of goals they want to achieve. A minimalist life has a clear purpose. To do this, you need to discover the few things that interest you most and dedicate yourself to them.

- Taking care of body and mind: health is the starting point for feeling good. Therefore, it is essential to take care of yourself on two levels: the physical and the mental. Physical activity, nutrition, and sleep are the three key elements in this regard.
- Cultivate Full Attention: Minimalist life requires a quiet mind and that means being free from contradictory thoughts and in tune with the present moment. Practicing mindfulness or meditation for full attention helps to recover a peaceful state of consciousness. You will be able to observe your thoughts and feelings without judging them, resisting them, feeding them, and consciously responding to situations, instead of overreacting or being exhausted by them.

www.ingramcontent.com/pod-product-compliance
Lightning Source LLC
Chambersburg PA
CBHW072200100526
44589CB00015B/2297